CONSCIOUS LEADERS

CONSCIOUS LEADERS

For Futures That Are Sustainable

CHUTISA BOWMAN

With Major Contribution from
GARY DOUGLAS
and
STEVEN BOWMAN

ACCESS CONSCIOUSNESS PUBLISHING

Published by
Access Consciousness Publishing, LLC
www.accessconsciousnesspublishing.com

Contents

CONSCIOUS LEADERS

Introduction

Brilliance, charm, persuasiveness, self-confidence, presence, the ability to communicate, and being business savvy are essential gifts for a leader, but they are no longer sufficient. Twenty-first century leadership faces an environment more erratic, precarious, and unpredictable than ever. As the speed of change quickens, more and more leaders are finding themselves unable to navigate these arduous changes and unfamiliar landscapes. Real progress in the decade ahead will require different, creative, generative, strategically aware, and conscious leaders.

This book is an invitation to a different possibility—the possibility of something you may never even have considered. This book is for people who are ready and open to the choice of new possibilities and to the question of what can get created that is greater than what you have ever been able to create before.

Since early 2005, when my first book, *Conscious Leadership*, was published, the fields of conscious leadership and conscious business have grown and generated new levels of interest and excitement. The use of the terms "conscious business," "conscious leadership," and "conscious leader" in media and business has multiplied significantly. The fields of conscious leadership and conscious business have an immense possibility to initiate major changes across society and the world.

However, nearly fifteen years after my first book, the leadership paradigm has not evolved nearly as much as I knew could be possible. What happened? In retrospect, I was idealistic. The truth is that it is challenging for most people to wrap their minds around what being a conscious leader actually is. Integrating conscious awareness and personal power to lead in this reality proved far more challenging for most people than I had considered. Additionally, there are many people who are committed to their job but do not aspire to become conscious leaders. The aspiration for leadership is generally beyond their reality.

In this reality, we aren't taught about being conscious and leading with awareness. Instead, we get indoctrinated into living life according to the finite possibility of this reality. This reality requires us to be in a constant state of judgment and motion to create the context in which we fit, benefit, and win (or lose). Business training courses and leadership workshops offer frameworks that teach us to operate *within the context of this reality*. With these frameworks in place, we understand where we fit, where we can benefit, where we can win, and how to avoid losing. In effect, what we do is put on the filter of our conclusions, preconceptions, and biases.

For instance, when I was working as a principal ergonomist and usability specialist, I was trained to constantly engage in traditional competitive analysis, looking through the lens of our current business practices and industry structures to identify what might transpire in the near future. We conducted analysis through the filter of "the right way to do things." We judged the products' potential through the filter of industry lenses that are framed by past reference points. We had to look at thousands of things with respect to how they might be, how they should be, how they could be, or how they ought to be. We relied too much on the past for indications of right or wrong, or good or bad, and what might happen in the future.

These filters have one superficial purpose: to distinguish whether things are good or bad, or right or wrong, based on what has worked in the past. The filters lead us to think only about what *should* be created, thus separating us from opening to the choice of new possibility and to the question of what *can* be created. In my role as an ergonomist, it was hard to embody and be a conscious leader when we were always operating based on the construct of this reality.

Today, I advise business leaders that there is no such thing as right or wrong, or good or bad, when you are looking for different choices and different possibilities. There is no perfect answer or impeccable solution when you're looking for the next big thing to do. You've got to get to the place where you are willing to have total choice and total possibility with no point of view about how it shows up or what it looks like when it shows up. The ability to perceive and receive the possibility of something you have never even considered is the most important quality a leader can have.

A way of being, a mindset, an attitude.

There's no doubt that we all have the power to lead with conscious awareness. Being a conscious leader isn't just for people in the business world. It is also for individual development and growth in private life. It does not require an elite education; it requires a commitment to be, to live, and to be in action as a conscious leader. It is not about a few unique people making choices for everyone else. It is for everyone who has a desire to grow and expand beyond where they are today—beyond other people's points of view, beyond the ordinary, and beyond this contextual reality.

When you function based on contextual reality, you always try to put yourself in context with everything else. You are always trying to locate yourself in the structure of it. This is the space where you are constantly asking, "Where do I fit, where do I benefit, where do I win, and where do I lose?"

Conscious leaders can be found in a variety of positions in business, academia, non-profits, government—all fields and industries. They can be small business owners, entrepreneurs, corporate executives, CEOs, CFOs, managers, scientists, doctors, lawyers, teachers, IT specialists, pilots, chefs, farmers, consultants, parents, librarians, artists, designers, and many others.

My career has followed a pathway pretty typical of many corporate executives of my generation. In the early days of my work as a senior executive for a major corporation in Australia, I made a conscious choice to be an active and vibrant example of the power of commitment to lead with conscious awareness. I made this choice because I knew (and still know) that being a leader is not the same as acting as one, and calling myself a leader is not the same as being one. Conscious leadership goes beyond labels. When you take that stand and function from there, you take different action than when you believe that leadership is about controlling people or managing them to ensure that everything goes the way you want it to go.

In order to commit to lead with conscious awareness, I have learned to control my urge to micromanage. From the start of my leadership career, one of my biggest challenges was learning how to appropriately delegate. I used to struggle with delegation and often came off as micromanaging, leading my teams to feel over-scrutinized. To overcome my impulse to micromanage, I chose to see myself as a *facilitator* rather than a manager. I employed the power of awareness to facilitate my team and realize our objectives.

My most important responsibility as a leader and a facilitator was to heighten people's enthusiasm. However, enthusiasm, like trust, was not something I could command, control, or force people to have. I certainly couldn't stipulate a certain behavior or conduct. Conduct is determined by very distinct personal responses; people are not engaged or enthusiastic if they are forced to do work that isn't fun or meaningful to them. It became clear to me that, to be enthusiastic, the team must be more engaged—meaning that they had the chance to do what they did best every day. In that paradigm, enthusiasm was a choice!

When I catch myself having an urge to micromanage someone, one tactic I've used is asking questions. I chose to be the question and the energy to create a different possibility: *"What contribution can I be? What question can I ask? Is this a contribution to their work? What can I choose here? What can I be or do different today?"* I also remind myself to stop judging—to stop looking for the wrongness of what they chose.

I have found that people are more engaged when they have opportunities to learn and grow both personally and professionally. For the team to be fully engaged and willing to commit their time, talent, and energy in adding value to the team, they must clearly understand the vision and priorities and how they contribute to each. According to Antoine de Saint-Exupéry, the French pilot and poet, *"If you want to build a ship, don't drum up people to collect wood and don't assign them tasks and work, but rather teach them to long for the endless immensity of the sea."* It's all about the people's desire to have adventure, to have a sense of participation and contribution, to do work that's personally meaningful, and to really enjoy what they're doing every day.

I did not see my leadership responsibility as getting people to do what I wanted. Being a conscious leader is being an enabler who encourages and supports people to create a different possibility. I was willing to do anything in my power to position my staff for additional exciting projects, interesting clients, or invigorating roles. I showed my team that I trusted them by sharing what was important to me and why. I also made sure that I did what I said I would do.

I initiated total transparency and strong lines of open communication that flowed in all directions with my team. Together, we embodied the energy to create a different possibility. We set priorities, established targets, developed tactics, and set clear and easy to understand priorities. In my view, clear priorities determine strategies, guide actions, direct performance, and boost the enthusiasm of all the people involved.

The commitment to be a conscious leader influenced my life trajectory. I came to understand what commitment meant and discovered many things that have stood me in great stead ever since. Choosing to be a conscious leader isn't a job or a whim or a status symbol or a political statement. It's an expression of my own staunch commitment to living a life without limitation.

Being a conscious leader is a way of being, a mindset, an attitude, and an outlook that must be ever-present in your energy, space, consciousness, and awareness. It isn't something you do once and then sit back and relax. You have to continually choose to be, to live, to act, and to function from the space that would create the greatest future possibilities. This is where you choose from possibility, where you create from possibility, and where you have infinite possibility. I have found that when I lead my life with conscious awareness, each day brings multiple possibilities. It is not about success but about the possibilities I am creating. It is about the moment when I know that the things I've done will change something.

When you recognize that conscious leadership can be used to create a different reality—without having the sense that anyone else needs to understand, see, or follow what you are doing—you can create beyond this reality with great ease. And, when you know with certainty that conscious leadership is a creative factor for a greater possibility, you engage in your work in a more generative way.

Open the doors to everything you are capable of!

The changes that are taking place globally are unprecedented in their scope. They are generating unlimited opportunities and unrestrained threats. In the next decade, leaders and businesses must embrace the capacity to truly function from a high level of consciousness and strategic awareness. Failure to do so will result in futures that are not sustainable; it will suppress progress at a period when progress is essential.

As a leader, if you're not choosing to lead with conscious awareness, it will be hard for your business or your life to grow. When you truly function from a high level of consciousness, you start opening the door to creating from a different place—and a different possibility begins to come to life. This is where you choose from possibility, where you create from possibility, and where you have infinite possibility.

When you become a conscious leader and truly lead with strategic awareness, you perceive choices and possibilities you never knew were available. You open the doors to everything you are capable of when you choose to be conscious. Suddenly, different choices and different possibilities open up.

Twenty years ago, when I heard the statement, "Never live your life by other people's points of view," it was merely words. Now that I am able to fully embrace and be a conscious leader in my own life, I know that this advice is one of the most important decrees of conscious leadership. It's so important that I've devoted the bulk of one chapter later in the book to it.

The first element of conscious leadership is making a commitment to be a leader of your life. When I first made a commitment to my life, I opened the doors to everything I was capable of being and doing. I perceived choices and possibilities I never knew existed and began to recognize *what I was about*, which allowed me to have more creative exploration.

The breakthrough discovery I made about myself was that, above all else, I wanted to be liked and did not want to be judged. As a result, I sacrificed being myself for being liked. I kept looking for what other people were doing and spent a fair portion of my life holding in place a major facade about things. Taking ownership and making a commitment to my life was the first step toward reducing and eliminating my need to be liked.

I became aware that my desire to be liked by everyone was holding me back from what I could be, what I could choose, and what I could create. What I was not willing to receive was that which kept me from being the greatness I could truly be. In order to have the life I desired, I had to be willing to receive everything just as it was—in every moment of every day—and stop looking for things to be different.

From that awareness, I made a conscious choice to expand my willingness to receive judgment with ease. Willingness to receive judgment doesn't mean that I don't care when people judge me; it's about the willingness to face the judgment fully without a point of view and without flinching. I still care when people judge me, but I don't choose to get involved with their judgment or buy it as real.

I actually find it very challenging to ignore what other people say, but now, instead of taking it personally, I simply say, "Isn't that interesting!" It doesn't matter what their judgments of me are, I just remind myself that judgments are not real. I choose to be in allowance.

Recognizing judgments as interesting points of view is a choice I have. I'm treating every judgment and other people's disapproval as just an interesting point of view.

However, I also recognize that in order to continue to grow and create a life that works for me, I have to believe in my own abilities, whether anybody else sees them or not. I learned over time that while it was very challenging to purge feelings of doubt and hesitation, I had to be willing to see it as a possibility. When I felt like I was not capable of doing something, I asked myself this question: "What am I capable of, that if I would acknowledge it, would give me all the possibilities I believe I do not have?" Taking initiative pays off.

When I changed my point of view and committed to me, to my life, to my awareness, and to becoming a conscious leader, I became a creator of my life and my reality. I am willing to be that leader and go where I am going—whether anybody else goes along or not.

Committing to conscious leadership is so powerful that, when you do it, you become part of creating futures that are sustainable for you and the world. Creating futures that are sustainable can't be taken for granted. The future is too precious to be left to chance. Futures that are truly sustainable must be created day by day, choice by choice, action by action, and leader by leader.

Creating futures that are sustainable takes awareness, confidence, and boldness. It also takes the discipline to tune out negative voices that try to convince you to live your life by other people's points of view and to do what everybody else says is right for you.

The key is to make a choice to be a conscious leader who goes forward—whether anybody goes with you or not—intent on expanding your ability to lead with conscious awareness and to cultivate new possibilities. The need for conscious leadership capabilities is greater than ever, and these concerns must be at the center of how leaders think about their businesses.

The main source of your generative advantage will be your leadership capabilities, your culture, and the operating strategy of your organization. This book presents different ways of thinking about leadership that will encourage you to lead your business and your life in a different way. We will talk about what it takes to actually develop your capacities to be a conscious leader—to become a catalyst for different possibilities and to transform the world for the better. This is not theory or academia. In the world of conscious leadership, understanding what it really takes can only come from people who practice what they preach and are out there every day doing what we talk about in this book.

This book builds on our personal experiences, our involvement in business, and our work with individuals and organizations. It is based on the awareness that conscious leadership skills and competencies are needed to meet the demands of today's business world and of everyday life and living.

ONE

A Different Possibility
Is Available to You

Most people are not educated to function from a high level of consciousness or to lead with awareness, let alone create futures that are sustainable. They are trained to fit into this contextual reality. Conventional leadership training is not enough if you are to thrive and create futures that are sustainable. You must also have conscious leadership skills. If you know how to lead with conscious awareness, regardless of your particular enterprise, your age, or your personal circumstances, you have a much greater chance of succeeding, growing a larger life and business, and skyrocketing.

Tragically, many leaders and businesses, large and small, still operate their businesses at the expense of societal, cultural, environmental, physical, and emotional well-being. Many still choose to operate with a high level of anti-conscious practices and a major lack of awareness of their overall impact on society and the planet. They are blissfully unaware and tend to go about their daily affairs without questioning anything.

These businesses ask, "Where's my share of the pie?" rather than, "How can I create beyond this?" Too many business leaders have the point of view that the world is set up so they have to get their share or others will take it away. Do you see how much unconsciousness is attached to this viewpoint?

One of the challenges facing leaders today is that the business environment is undergoing exponential change. Never before has the landscape been changing so rapidly and the industry boundaries becoming so malleable. Some leaders find their capacity and agility challenged when confronting situations that violate and defy their expectations of how things should be. For example, some leaders are overwhelmed or baffled when business conditions shift or the marketplace takes a turn that the strategic plan didn't foresee. They can't cope with circumstances beyond their ability to predict, so they either overreact or become paralyzed.

Xerox is a good example of a business that became baffled when conditions shifted. The senior executives at Xerox saw it as a successful technology company, but others saw it as a copier company. In the early 1970s, Xerox decided it wanted to become a leader in the information systems and data processing business. By 1975, and after millions of dollars, Xerox Data Systems was killed. In 1979, Xerox tried to get into the facsimile business with its Telecopier line of products, but with little success.

Xerox invented laser printing, a technology close to its original core business. The company should have owned the computer laser printer market, but they ignored the trend and allowed HP to step in and own the market. In 1984, HP introduced the LaserJet at $3,500 and sold 10,000 units in three months. Today, more copies are made from laser printers than from Xerox's photocopying machines. Failure to recognize trends and opportunities beyond an organization's primary area of business results in missed opportunities. The downfall of Xerox is a result of technological change and leadership failure. Xerox's leaders became derailed, and the injury and dysfunction that they set in motion has been devastating for that business.

There have been increasing incidents of executive derailment, where executives engage in behaviors that cause harm to themselves and their organizations. Like train derailment, executive derailment usually comes as a surprise to everyone, including the executives themselves. Business executives who derail have a number of common characteristics: difficulty adapting and changing, problems with interpersonal relationships, inability to build and lead a team, failure to meet organizational objectives, and an overly operational focus that discounts the importance of strategic positioning.

The truth is that most business executives are struggling in the face of today's challenges, unable to adapt and change quickly enough. Unless you are willing to radically change the way you function in the world and become more multifaceted, you are likely to become derailed.

What if there's a different possibility for leading and creating?

There is! It's *conscious leadership.* Any person on this Earth can make the choice to become a conscious leader. It's not a matter of luck, destiny, or circumstance, but a direct outcome of making some essential changes in your outlook and your life. If you wish to become a conscious leader for futures that are sustainable, but you don't know what it would take for that to transpire, this book will inspire you to see different possibilities and point you toward creating sustainable futures.

Many people, in their first encounters with conscious leadership, get stuck on the word *conscious*. Literally! *Conscious* means "the ability to be present in your life in every moment." *Conscious* also means recognizing that we are connected to the energy of all creation. You may find this difficult to comprehend. Actually, it's not feasible to fully grasp the meaning of the word. That's the point! Any definition of it isn't really it. It's undefinable, unconfinable, indescribable, and infinitely present, and it flows through all things. It's not something to believe in. It's what and who you are.

I have learned that no one can teach you how to become conscious; no one can teach you to function with awareness and to embody and be the greatness that you can truly be. Being a conscious leader is practiced as a personal transformation. It's not about acquiring consciousness as capacities or possessions but rather simply becoming more conscious and aware. Being conscious is not to have; it is to be.

One of my early and important lessons about consciousness and conscious leadership was in my work with Conscious Governance. My husband Steve and I created Conscious Governance in 2003 to facilitate board directors to function with strategic awareness and to appreciate their accountability for the performance of their organizations. We discovered that large numbers of board directors were not aware of the immense possibilities and the dynamic effects truly conscious boards and conscious leaders could have on businesses and the world.

People ask, "What's required for me to be conscious?" I say, "Choice. You just have to choose it." Here's the thing: If you choose to be a conscious leader and you truly choose to live with awareness, you will have a different way of functioning. You will have the capacity to enjoy everything in life. The choice instantly changes how you see yourself, and your priorities will shift in fundamental ways. With consciousness you will be aware of everything in totality. Total awareness does not necessarily give you a comfortable reality, of course. It just gives you a lot of awareness, which allows you to shape your life rather than be shaped by it.

In what proved to be a turning point for me, I had the privilege to listen to a preeminent conscious business leader, Gary Douglas (founder of Access Consciousness, a global business in over 130 countries). In the early 2000s, Gary spoke about being conscious and what is possible beyond this reality. He extrapolated on the energetics of the limitations impelled at us—daily, continuously, constantly. He invited us to recognize that every limitation is a possibility we haven't yet considered.

Gary later became my mentor and friend, but the first time I heard him speak I knew him simply as a gifted virtuoso of consciousness—a global business leader, best-selling author, international speaker, and sought-after facilitator—who was giving a series of workshops around the world for Access Consciousness. I sat in the front row, captivated by this incredibly expressive and eloquent presenter speaking with great exuberance. He offered insight and awareness about a different way of looking at the world. His presentation was not just erudite, not just generative, but, for me, completely transformative, eye-opening, and life-changing.

I was riveted by Gary's talk and the questions he was asking, but the one that changed my life was this: "You are the source for creating the change you desire," he said. "But you have to be willing to be it. *What would it be like if you embodied so much consciousness in everything you did that others chose to become more conscious as a result?*" This question was a spark of inspiration for me. I knew instantly that this was exactly what I desired to be.

I truly wanted to create a different reality. I asked Gary, "What can I choose or what can I do differently?" He said, "It's not about doing something differently. It's about how you can *choose* to be different and create a different reality for you."

There are a whole lot of changes going on with the earth, Gary said, and we need to access this energy, this awareness we have. We need to be prepared to *be* the energy that can change everything and everyone around us, so that chaos and mayhem are not the standard by which people function in the future. I considered the possibility of what he was saying; his comment moved me deeply. For me, this was the moment of potent and insightful affirmation of something I had been aware of for some time, and he was voicing it. That moment of powerful awareness has never left me. I began to acknowledge what was actually true for me and recognize what I would like to create.

I became completely committed to creating and generating a different way forward—one that would create change in the world and in people's lives. At some level, this life commitment stemmed from Gary's example of the generative and the benevolent way he had chosen to create his life and his business. He facilitated my understanding that *I* am the source for creating the change I desire, creating a life that goes beyond the limitations of what the rest of the world thinks is important. It was from this awareness that I set out to discover what it would take to embody and be a conscious leader in my own life and in the world.

I knew that there was much more to life and to business than what those around me chose. I became aware of the catalyst I could be for a different possibility in the world. It was the "Wow" moment of my life—a spontaneous awareness of what *can* be generated. Realizing this, my question became, "What can I be, do, have, create, or generate to actualize this?" This set up a new idea: the possibility of conscious leadership in motion.

Conscious leadership is an essential aspect to creating a future that has greater possibilities for everyone and the planet. This is a priority for all—not only for businesses but for personal happiness and for creating futures that are sustainable. If enough people choose to become conscious leaders, to be more aware and more conscious, we will start to see the possibilities of what we have available and to change what is occurring here on planet Earth.

Being conscious isn't a concept. It's not some kind of far-fetched, supernatural imagining. It's not spiritual or religious. You can be conscious and aware and not have a spiritual or religion context. Even though it's not tangible, it is always present, always with you. Being a conscious leader is the essential you—if you are choosing to claim, own, and acknowledge it.

If you choose to be a conscious leader and truly have consciousness, you will enjoy everything in life. With consciousness you will be aware of everything in totality. True enjoyment is possible. Remember, though, that total awareness does not necessarily give you a comfortable reality all the time. It just gives you a lot of awareness.

The key is who you choose to be!

Consciousness is an open-ended space where anything becomes possible, everything is available, and the choices you make determine how you are willing to be with yourself and everybody around you. Consciousness is never what you think it's going to be, only what it is. When conscious, you have a sense of possibility, expansion, and gratitude—a sense of peace and joy for everything and everyone around you—because you are present in your life in every moment. Consciousness is only a choice away. It's a choice you have to make.

Across the world, we see too many intense business predicaments and dilemmas of governance, showing that all is not healthy at the top of many public, private, and non-profit enterprises. Numerous directors and CEOs have been accused of failing in their duties. This is a global concern.

These shortcomings occur because leaders tend to focus on managing for short-term outcomes. Consequently, they underplay leading with conscious awareness. They don't create a place where they are in a constant state of creation. They function from the constructs and limitations of the past instead of showing the way ahead and being conscious leaders.

Traditional leadership training is not enough if you are to generate different possibilities and thrive in this tumultuous business world. You must also have conscious leadership skills and awareness. If you have the ability to be present in your life in every moment, regardless of your particular interest or enterprise, you have a much greater chance to succeed and generate futures that are sustainable for your life, your business, and the world. Otherwise, you will most likely become obsolete.

Being a conscious leader and expanding the ability to generate your life with conscious awareness has nothing to do with education, intelligence, work habits, luck, business expertise, or choice of jobs. The key is who you choose to be. It isn't something you do once and then sit back and relax; it is a commitment to constantly choosing to embody and be the greatness that you truly are.

You must make a demand of yourself to be everything you can possibly be regardless of anyone or anything. If you choose to be a conscious leader, you have to embody these energies. It is your choice.

There is a completely different reality available to you if you are willing to choose to be the greatness that you truly are. Making a choice to be a conscious leader is the place where you realize that the way people function and lead according to this reality is not enough for you. You would like to create something different.

The more you choose to embody and be the energy, space, and consciousness of a conscious leader, the more of the unconscious or anticonscious aspects of your life will dissipate. You will begin to seize infinite choice and infinite possibilities, to live each precious moment fully and with gusto.

―――――

What would it be like to be a conscious leader
for futures that are sustainable?

―――――

Being a conscious leader for futures that are sustainable is about the recognition that you have the power and capacity to create a different reality. It is the recognition of *how you can be the energy that changes things.* Every choice you make determines what your future can be. When you make a choice, recognize what limitations are being generated with that choice.

By sustainable, I'm not just talking "survive." I'm talking about where the future actually grows and becomes something that is truly greater. This means that each and every one of us must contribute to making the future better than it would have been without us. It means that we should enrich the world by our existence and create value for everyone we touch.

Your choice is what creates your future!

Although the future is unknown and has yet to happen, it's crucial to recognize that your choice is what creates your future. Your choices and actions compound and have an effect on what the future will be. What creates the future is what you do today, in the present moment. This requires conscious choice and consideration about what you desire to create as your future.

You need to ask the questions, *"What is the future that will be created many years from now by the choice I make today? What do we have to be and do today to generate sustainable futures?"*

The key to creating futures that are sustainable is acknowledging that you are shaping the future by the choices and actions you are making day-by-day, in the course of living your life and doing your job. This is vital information. Many of us don't realize or consider that we are making our future, for better or worse, by the choices we make and by what we do each day. All choices and actions are open-ended to the future. So, the choices and actions you take now have compound effects for your future.

No future is solid. Every future is malleable and changeable, which is why we talk about sustainable futures. Every time you make a choice it creates multiple future possibilities. It includes effects that are unpredictable; you don't know the ways they will play out in the future. In an open-ended sense, it could be that your choices and your actions generate a chain of events even more unpredictable and risky than if you had done nothing.

The future is not about completion. It is not about getting it the way we want, nor is it about playing it safe. Instead of avoiding risk, conscious leaders have the willingness to bring awareness to how our choices are going to impact our future. A few years ago, I made a choice to create the "Conscious Leaders" project. I didn't attempt to define what the project was going to be, and I didn't even plan to write the first book, let alone this book. I was in a constant state of question, choice, and possibility. I was asking, "What is going to create the greatest possibility here for everyone?" I wasn't trying to define what I wanted to create, or what I wanted to do, or what I wanted to generate, or how I wanted it to look, or any of that.

I realized that the future for this project could only begin with the willingness to be the contribution, the catalyst, and the source for creating a different future. This could only be achieved by being the curiosity of possibilities and choice. It's not about defining the future with conclusion, projection, and expectation. I didn't contract myself to create the future that I saw or the future I decided ought to be. I just had to *be* in the moment and pose the questions, *"What else is possible?"* and *"What is the future that will be created by the choice I make today?"*

These questions led to multiple possibilities beyond what I had ever considered. These possibilities showed up as face-to-face master classes, online induction programs for business executives, and an online training program for high school seniors around the world, which led to creating a graphic novel about conscious leaders and further events and resources for education. This has created a mini-business in the education sector. Another possibility that came into being was a conscious leaders program utilizing horses to facilitate exponentially raising levels of awareness and insights. These have all now been created and have been running as successful businesses around the world for a number of years.

Future is about awareness.

Creating a future is about creating possibilities from awareness and conscious choice. Again, it's not about defining the future that you have decided *ought* to be. Once you recognize this simple point, it becomes easier to make a paradigm shift from creating the future as a solidity, to creating the future as an energy.

From this new awareness, by being the curiosity of possibilities and choice, you can choose to be the source for creating a sustainable future. You begin by choosing to be the energy, space, and consciousness of the future you desire to be. Don't judge what you think ought to be and stop trying to define it. Ask, *"If I were creating my future today, what would I choose right away? What would I like to choose?"*

Creating futures that are sustainable entails recognizing that you are the generator for everything in your life. You must acknowledge that you cannot fully tell what the future will bring. Indeed, you can try to affect it, which is where the idea of creating futures that are sustainable comes in. A future is not predictable and there is a high degree of uncertainty, so it may be futile to make predictions, especially to make important decisions based on those predictions. Rarely can the future be predicted by simply extending current trajectories.

An interesting example of this is RadioShack. In the pre-Internet days, RadioShack reigned supreme in electronics, but the company failed to effectively adapt its model and missed almost every opportunity to be the center of the technology revolution. Some of these involved failing to spot up-and-coming competition, such as Amazon, while others included confused marketing strategies and a poor mix of inventory. With products that are easily sold through online channels, brick-and-mortar electronics retailers have been among the most vulnerable to Amazon. The company declared bankruptcy in 2017, following a prior bankruptcy filing in 2015. They closed 1,000 stores, leaving just 70 company-owned stores still open along with 500 dealer-owned stores. While the brand still exists today, it's a mere shell of its former self.

The RadioShack example confirms that the future will be different from what exists now and from what we expect. Too often, leaders and companies operate on a differing assumption: They attempt to define what the future is going to be and then try to control the outcomes to be what they expect.

When leaders and businesses function from a belief in the *ideal* future (based on conclusions, projections, expectations, and judgments), they believe they must define the future or they won't be able to control it. Control is trying to figure everything out and getting everyone to do it the way they want them to do it. They define the limitations and come to conclusion about which choice will create the outcome they desire. They have eliminated the possibility of any future greater than what is controllable for them.

Business is now at a turning point.

Economies have entered a new era. We live in a time of accelerating change in the global landscape. Globalization, environmental calamities, technological advances, and other complex forces are buffeting us like never before. To prosper and thrive in the decades ahead, leaders have to think differently about the way they live their life and lead their business. Yet most leaders do everything they can to keep their timeworn conventional business models in place.

In the book *Billion Dollar Lessons*, Paul Carroll and Chunka Mui reveal that since 1981, 423 U.S. companies with assets of more than $500 million filed for bankruptcy. Their combined assets at the time of the bankruptcy filings totaled more than $1.5 trillion. What caused all those failures? Various reasons and justifications have been given.

Many of these leaders concluded that their collapse was due to forces beyond their influence and power. From our observation, however, everything boiled down to their powerlessness to adapt. They failed to recognize and deal with spasmodic change or act on the risks and opportunities. Many of the companies that filed bankruptcy did not see that they were about to become obsolete—until it was too late. They failed to grasp the ways in which globalization, changes in technology, environmental emergencies, and the new hyper-changing world could restructure their industries. In most cases, they couldn't fathom that their organization's existence could be threatened.

These leaders demonstrated that failing to consciously create futures that are sustainable can destroy organizations. When leaders are operating unconsciously, they tend to demonstrate a precarious lack of awareness, short-sightedness of vision, and superficiality in their priorities. These leaders operate from a fixed idea of how things are supposed to be, rather than being present in the moment, where they are aware of everything, which allows them to perceive different possibilities.

Great prospects and new possibilities in business always come from changes that are taking place right here and right now. Every day brings new possibilities, new risks, and new challenges. It brings requirements to do things that you did not think you would have to do. If you are blinded by the norms of conventional practice or fixed points of view, you won't see the changes until it's too late. Setbacks are certain to emerge when leaders focus primarily on conventional practices.

The most effective way to create futures that are sustainable is to *create* them. As a leader, you must become a creator of different futures by embodying and being a conscious leader, by implementing the elements of leading consciously today in order to create futures that are sustainable tomorrow. It is *being the energy of these futures* that allows for a different possibility. If you are willing to be conscious, you can change anything. Without consciousness, you can't get there.

When you are willing to *be* the energy of the futures that are sustainable, you will receive the whispers of the future. When you function from question, choice, possibility, and contribution, you will become aware of something in the wind that is whispering change that you cannot fathom. They are the whispers of a future that has never been. When you are willing to listen to the whispers of the future, the future you desire can show up with ease.

Question, choice, possibility, and contribution are the four elements of how you can create anything. Here's how Gary Douglas explains it: "You create your reality. When you go into question, you open the door to choices. Choice is what creates. Every choice creates

an awareness, which creates another set of possibilities. Every possibility opens a door to another question and another choice. Contribution
is what you give and how you receive at the same time. It's the simultaneity of gifting and receiving. When you function from question,
choice, possibility, and contribution, every choice creates many future
possibilities, not a single result."

TWO

What Leaders Need Now Is Conscious Leadership

Leadership skills and business acumen are often overestimated and regularly misconstrued. When people achieve success, they often explain their achievements by simply attributing everything to their skills as a business leader. But this is a misleading and incorrect way of looking at leadership capacity.

Many people in business believe that they can become leaders in their organization or field of expertise because of their extensive experience in the field, superior technical knowledge, and excellent process management skills. This is often not the case. Leadership skill and business acumen are not enough.

Please note that I am not dismissing the importance of business skills and acumen here. I recognize that business skills and acumen are imperative for any business and should be cherished and appreciated.

Business skills and acumen can enable people to do remarkable things, and it gives entrepreneurs a head start on others. What separates the ordinary, run-of-the-mill businesses from the generatively thriving ones are the leaders of those businesses.

These leaders have the ability to see the world through different eyes. They operate with greater awareness of new possibilities; they see things that others miss. These are the capacities that differentiate people like Sheryl Sandberg, Sir Richard Branson, and Howard Schultz from others. They have the drive, commitment, awareness, and energy to lead their business to new possibilities. Sheryl Sandberg of Facebook, aside from being business- and tech-savvy, has spent most of her career advocating for women and speaking out about the importance of giving women equal opportunities to thrive. Sir Richard Branson of Virgin Group exemplifies that true success is the ability to be driven by something greater than money. Howard Schultz of Starbucks is a consummate example of courage, hard work, and the ability to turn obstacles into different possibilities.

Early in people's careers, business skills and acumen separate start-up entrepreneurs from the rest of the pack. However, too many people who start with good business acumen often lose their lead because they don't have leadership capacity. They rely on their business skills alone instead of choosing to cultivate their ability to lead with conscious awareness. They assume that business skills alone will keep them out front.

In addition, most standard business training programs focus exclusively on skills. These programs develop managers rather than leaders. Traditional business models seek to preserve the status quo and make good "soldiers" of the team. These models are based in authority, hierarchy, exclusivity, and separation between management and staff. It is important to recognize that it is just not feasible or generative to push and control other people to behave a certain way.

It's not a matter of chance, it's a matter of choice.

The role of leadership in business is coming under increasing scrutiny with calls for more accountability in governance at the executive and board levels. Seldom has a week gone by without a media report of a business that has self-destructed, been called to account for alleged inappropriate use of assets, or criticized publicly due to perceived lack of leadership. Never before have the consequences of the top leaders' anti-conscious behavior and short-sightedness been more destructive or upsetting.

The question remains: What generates the competence essential for engendering a truly thriving business? It comes from who you choose to be. *Choosing* to be a leader who functions from conscious awareness will set you apart from others who have good business skills and acumen alone. Ability to lead with conscious awareness is not a matter of chance; it is a matter of choice. It is not a thing to be waited for; it is something that you have to choose to embody and be—not just to wishfully think about but actually *choose* to be.

Leading with conscious awareness is a matter of choice!

In today's environment of dynamic continuous change, constant disruption, and genuine transparency, *conscious awareness* is a critical component of business agility and growth. Leading with conscious awareness is a matter of choice. Every choice you make from consciousness and awareness makes you a conscious leader.

If you are choosing to be a conscious leader for your business, then you are never going to eliminate or disengage awareness to create something. You are always going to incorporate awareness to create something greater. Awareness is the only thing that will grow anything for your business and your life. Business leaders who lack conscious awareness and acuity to see new possibilities get derailed sooner, while the injuries they cause due to their ineffectiveness can be astounding.

Change and disruption can come from left field and be very abrupt. Potentially great organizations are crippled by leaders who refuse to be aware of the new hyper-changing world and continue to manage their business as usual. There are not only massive disruptions but also great threats that can extinguish whole companies and industries. The disruption can be brutal, and leaders who can't or don't adapt are often finding their business models challenged and even shredded. Business leaders must constantly keep an eye on the big picture; they must keep evolving in the face of rapid change and disruption—or risk becoming extinct. In case you don't believe this could apply to you and your business, the following examples show this belief can turn disruption into failure no matter what industry you work in!

Four of the best examples of this are the Polaroid Corporation, Blockbuster, Bang & Olufsen, and Kodak. The Polaroid Corporation was a pioneer in digital imaging in the 1960s. The company did not make the necessary investments to hold that lead in the 1990s, when digital photography overtook film. Blockbuster was once the industry leader in video rentals, but the company became stagnant, failing to respond to the growing popularity of video-on-demand services and video rental kiosks. It held on to an outmoded business model just long enough to fail. Bang & Olufsen was once the eminent Danish luxury electronics purveyor, well known for their distinctive design appeal. This company was so committed to following its own path that it chose to ignore the disruption happening around it. It was forced to shed product lines and lay off hundreds of workers because the leaders closed their eyes to forewarning indications and they were not willing to break with their own conventional practices. Bang &

Olufsen failed to keep up with consumers who had been switching from bulky stereo systems in their living rooms to portable music players and headphones. Kodak was the illustrious company that dominated the photography industry. For decades, Kodak's technology was untouchable. But Kodak didn't respond as digital technology emerged, and the company is now a shell of what it once was.

What confronts every business, large or small, today and in the years ahead, is not merely the challenge of dynamic, continuous change and constant disruption but knowing what it will take to respond to these changes as consciously and skillfully as required. The sheer difficulty of keeping a corporation afloat in such a turbulent environment is beyond most leaders' experience and capacity.

The rate of change in the business world today is greater than many leaders' ability to respond. Leaders will be constantly tested for their ability to lead in the midst of a crisis, make generative decisions, take advantage of different possibilities, and make the business better off than it was before.

Business acumen and experience are not sufficient in today's environment. There are many things that can hinder leaders from making sound decisions and taking effective action. That's where awareness and consciousness magnify leadership power. Leaders must cultivate the ability to both be and do, to lead their businesses in the most challenging business environment ever.

That's why today's companies require conscious leaders—leaders who are willing to commit to becoming the catalyst for a different possibility in the world. These are leaders who are capable of changing the world and changing the people around them. In my observation, leaders who are capable of changing the world are the people who go forward with consciousness whether anybody goes with them or not. They know what they want to be and do professionally and personally. They have the strength to continue in the face of setbacks, even failures. They are the greatest creators of value in the world.

So, how do you become a creator of value in the world? The key is making a commitment to your life. All of the remarkable leaders I have talked with confirmed that no one can teach you how to make a commitment to your life; no one can teach you to become the catalyst for a different possibility. No one except you. These leaders had to overcome an almost overwhelming series of difficulties in a variety of ways, but all emphasized the importance of making a commitment to their lives. Some start the practice early, and some postponed it until later.

I also learned that truly making a commitment to my life is sometimes anything but easy. As a child, I struggled to appreciate myself, know myself, and be myself, and I continued to struggle throughout my early adult life. In other words, I knew that I was not realizing my own potential and not being myself fully, but I hadn't been willing to be something different. It wasn't until Gary Douglas asked me, "Is there something you have as a capacity that you were not acknowledging?" and "What would you have to acknowledge about you that would allow you to truly commit to your own life?" that I began to fully acknowledge my capacities and my gift.

I became aware that EXTRAPOLATION is one of my greatest gifts and innate abilities, yet I didn't value it because it does not conform with the way people operate in this reality. Faced with this insight, I realized that what I had been doing and choosing to attain was not truly what I would really like to create as my life. There was something awe-inspiring about that realization.

My first step toward change and new possibility was to acknowledge that I am a dynamic extrapolator. An extrapolator is one who takes the elements of things and figures out how they can be used to create a different possibility. A dynamic extrapolator can take new information and expand it into multiple possibilities and come up with something that didn't exist before. This acknowledgment of me was the turning point where I began to make a real commitment to my life. My business started to turn in a different direction. I was able to receive and perceive great new ideas and from that generate something that I hadn't considered before—which then allowed something else to come into existence. I started to create me as the gift and the contribution for a different possibility.

Until you truly commit to your life, you can succeed only in the most superficial sense of the word. When you commit to your life, you are willing to be, do, have, create, and generate anything in order to create greater for you, the world, and everyone concerned. This is very vital to a leader, because leading is not simply having a strategic vision, or giving orders, or showing the way. To become the catalyst for a different possibility in the world, you must commit to your life first and become the creator source of your own life.

The creation of new innovations, the ability for societies to move forward to create even greater possibilities in the world, and the increasing knowledge of how to interact with each other and the world generally are the greatest value-added activities of many conscious leaders.

Leaders need *conscious awareness* to create a culture of conscious innovation within organizations. Conscious systems and strategic awareness are essential for organizational effectiveness and future sustainability. Leaders also need it for themselves, as they must be able to operate in challenging, unpredictable circumstances.

There are a whole lot of changes going on in the business world.

As a business leader, you need to access this energy and awareness you have. You need to be prepared to be the energy that can change everything and everyone around you, so that mayhem is not the standard by which business and capitalism function in the future.

Gary Douglas has said, "People are capable of changing the world and changing the people around them with the energy they can be. If you walk into a room full of panic-stricken people, that panic can go away by your energy if you are willing to be it. But you have to be willing to be so potent that nothing stops the consciousness you are."

To thrive consistently over the long haul in an increasingly unsettling and chaotic world requires discipline and a reliable strategy for dealing with new opportunities and unforeseen adversities. The future of your organization and the world depends, in part, on how well you, the business leader, can function with conscious awareness, embrace social responsibility, demonstrate conscious leadership, maximize the power of your talent, and anticipate future possibilities.

A different reality is available to you if you're willing to have it. Please know that choosing a limitation is a choice—not a necessity.

THREE

What Is a Conscious Leader?

The buzz words for people doing any kind of personal development work right now are "conscious" and "consciousness." There are almost as many definitions of "conscious" and "consciousness" as there are people using the words. Evidently, they mean different things to different people.

Ask a group of people exactly what "conscious" means and you will get answers such as "wakeful," "alert," "awake," "mindful," and "responsive of one's surroundings." At a rudimentary level, according to most people, consciousness is the fact of being awake and processing information. From a medical perspective, consciousness is assessed as a "level" ranging from coma at the low end to full alertness and purposeful responsiveness at the high end. Doctors judge people as being conscious or not depending on their wakefulness and how they respond to external stimuli.

From a spiritual perspective, consciousness frequently implies the relationship between the mind and God, or the connection between the mind and Divinity. However, to most philosophers, the word *consciousness* represents the relationship between the mind and the world, and it is part of what allows us to exist and understand ourselves in the world. Some philosophers consider the state of being conscious as the connection between the being and the deeper truths (which are thought to be more fundamental than the physical world).

Being conscious may seem like a nebulous concept. For many decades, consciousness as a research topic was avoided by most mainstream scientists. The general feeling was that a phenomenon defined in subjective terms could not be properly studied using objective experimental methods.

Many people think that being a conscious leader means being virtuous, mindful, and ethical, creating value for the organization's stakeholders, and being sensible for the purpose of doing good. Or, as the expression goes, seeking to do well by doing good.

The truth is that being a conscious leader isn't about being noble or ethical. It's not about being altruistic. There's nothing lofty about it. It has nothing to do with self-important concepts. Being a conscious leader is about something much more pragmatic. It's about creating greater possibilities for yourself, your community, and the world at large. It's about the possibilities you are creating.

The choice to become a conscious leader is not limited to those who have leadership or management positions in large corporations. We all have a leadership role to play in today's world. Many people think the word *leader* only applies to those who have positions in corporations and businesses. They don't see individuals as leaders—but this is not accurate. We need conscious leaders to create sustainable futures and a sustainable planet, whether they are corporate executives, business owners, single mothers, doctors, teachers, students, entertainers, gardeners, or janitors.

Here's to the crazy ones. The ones who see things differently.

I can tell you almost to the day when I made the choice to become a conscious leader, the choice that changed my business and my life. In the early 2000s, I was a very successful corporate executive, responsible for a very large revenue stream, constantly traveling the world and managing a big team. A lot of people would fancy being in my position. But, something was missing for me. I was constantly wondering, *"Am I being all that I can be, and am I achieving all that I am capable of?"* and *"What am I really meant to do on this Earth, in this lifetime?"* I felt that there was more to me and what I could create and generate.

I've been a fan and admirer of Steve Jobs ever since I saw the famous "Think Different" television ad campaign that debuted in September 1997. It featured many remarkable leaders I admired, such as Mahatma Gandhi, Albert Einstein, Martin Luther King, Jr., Richard Branson, John Lennon, and Buckminster Fuller. The ad was anchored by the unforgettable "Crazy Ones" spot narrated by Richard Dreyfuss celebrating "the crazy ones . . . the ones who see things differently."

This "Think Different" ad campaign profoundly inspired me to see different possibilities that I had never considered. It changed my view on how I had been creating my reality. I became aware that I had been living my life by somebody else's reality. That's why I had been trying to figure out this question about the true meaning of life, time and time again.

I was so inspired by the text of the "Think Different" ad. The way it described these leaders incited, stirred, amused, and delighted me. And even more enthralling than the text was the lasting impact it had on the way I see the world.

Here's the text of the "Think Different" ad:

Here's to the crazy ones. The misfits. The rebels. The troublemakers. The round pegs in the square holes. The ones who see things differently.

They're not fond of rules and they have no respect for the status quo.

You can quote them, disagree with them, glorify or vilify them. About the only thing you can't do is ignore them. Because they change things.

They push the human race forward. And while some may see them as the crazy ones, we see genius.

Because the people who are crazy enough to think they can change the world are the ones who do.

All these incredible inspiring leaders, whether it's Steve Jobs or Martin Luther King, Jr., Mahatma Gandhi or Buckminster Fuller, all chose to create themselves as the source for creating a different world. They were willing to function at a bigger level than anybody else around them, which allowed them to create beyond the limitations of this reality. They were willing to be the leader and go where they were going, whether anybody else went along or not.

I never get tired of hearing Steve Jobs's incredible story and accomplishments. I have been studying the life and words of Steve Jobs since 1997, and one of the most important insights I received from him about business and leadership was this: "People who choose to be a catalyst for different possibilities, who see what it is they want to create in the world and act on them really can change the world . . . the work should be more than about improving your own self; it's about improving others' lives as well."

Go against the odds to create a difference.

Steve Jobs illustrated that if we are constantly choosing possibility, we can go beyond this reality with great ease. He lived his life by his reality. He was willing to have total choice and total possibility and go against the odds to create a difference. His commitment to being a catalyst for change and his drive for excellence in business continues to inspire me and the way I run my business.

A few years ago, I had an "aha" moment. I began to see that we all can create ourselves as the gift, as the possibility, and as the catalyst for a different reality. If we choose! More to the point, I became aware that if I was going to be the source for creating a different world, I had to be willing to function at a bigger level than anybody else around me. Now, every day I ask this question: *"What possibility do I have here that I have never considered?"*

It's been more than two decades since I first watched the "Think Different" television ad campaign. It still resonates with me today, many years after it ended. The ad campaign reinforces the key tenets of conscious leadership:

1. A conscious leader is willing to embody and be the greatness that they could truly be. They commit to being all that they can be. They don't cut off their awareness of themselves in order to be or live like other people.

2. A conscious leader commits to living a life without limitation, regardless of anything else. They are willing to go where they are going, whether anybody else goes along or not.

3. A conscious leader is always open to the choice of new possibilities and to the question of what can get created instead of concluding what should be created.

4. A conscious leader is a nonconformist even in the face of unfavorable consequences, with the courage to stand alone and the ability to effectively deal with uncertainty and risk.

5. A conscious leader has the ability to change and transform on a dime, willing to give up fixed expectations or predetermined outcomes and scrap a project when it doesn't lead to greater possibility.

6. A conscious leader doesn't see failures as mistakes and is not afraid to make mistakes. Mistakes are an opportunity for change, for growth, and for creating new and different possibilities.

One of the many interesting and appealing things about being conscious is that it's totally and completely internal. That is, it has nothing to do with anything or anyone else. It is a commitment you make to yourself not to live by anyone else's judgment and reality ever again, no matter what.

Look at the possibilities and not the problem.

Nothing is more destructive to our power to develop and expand our consciousness than to maintaining our fixed point of view about who we are. For example, if you have a fixed view that being a risk-taker is dangerous, if you have defined yourself as a sensible person—who is not extreme, who is risk-averse—then you will always seek middle ground and choose the most popular, innocuous ideas. Your life and your work may become average and ordinary. That's why I am so mindful about any fixed point of view. Any fixed point of view we take, any solidification of anything in our life, becomes the limitation of what we can be, do, have, create, and generate. We cannot create anything greater than our fixed point of view. We can undo the energetics of this limitation by looking at the possibilities and not the problem.

Consciousness is our intrinsic faculty and inner resource. Like any other intrinsic faculty, it can be strengthened through choice, practice, sincerity, and fortitude. Being conscious is an experience of expanding our awareness beyond its present limits. It is a state of flexible awareness, with no fixed points of view.

The key is "who you choose to be."

"Who you choose to be"—why is this relevant to leadership and business? Because who you choose to be, how you are in the world, creates your reality. Everyone is capable of being a conscious leader and creating a conscious business, but many times in our society, we are held back by one or more limitations that prevent us from realizing this capability. The limitations can vary. One common limitation is that we are instilled with a limiting belief that we can only achieve so much in our lives—and that there is nothing we can do about it.

This point of view often prevents us from finding the real greatness within ourselves. It leads us to choose paths that we manage to navigate well enough, but those paths really don't fulfill or satisfy us. Too often we just go through the motions of the tasks required by our job, just to obtain a paycheck in order to pay our expenses, support our lifestyle, and keep a roof over our heads. We've concluded, *"This is the way it is, this is the way I will always do it, and this is what's going to happen."*

If your intrinsic point of view is that *"I will never become a conscious leader,"* then it's absolute. You will not. If your thought is, *"I don't have the ability,"* then you will not choose to discover what it would take to develop the capacity.

Embody and be the greatness that you truly are.

"How do I become a truly conscious leader?" is a question I am asked often. Conscious leadership is a topic that often leaves even the most refined leadership experts baffled and perplexed. Cultivating the ability to be a conscious leader is a process of transformation and self-mastery on a personal level. It requires the same kind of genuine commitment that a business must undertake in achieving success and accomplishment.

Self-mastery requires harnessing the energy to embody and be *the greatness that you truly are.* To be the master of your own self is to be willing to commit to you—to create you as the gift, you as the possibility, and you as the contribution for a different reality, regardless of anything. The key is making a commitment to your life, to constant expansion of your consciousness and your awareness. What's required is not just a one-time improvement. More likely, you'll have to be adept at continually choosing and changing as you move forward.

Being *the greatness that you truly are* requires continuously choosing to be the possibility of something greater, something beyond what you have yet been willing to be. It's being willing to go beyond anything you have decided is you. If you are choosing to truly be a conscious leader, then making the choice to embody and be *the greatness that you truly are* is a minimum requirement.

What separates remarkable leaders from ordinary leaders is a total commitment and candid enthusiasm to doing whatever it takes to be the greatness that they truly are. This is the power that Elie Wiesel, Nobel Peace Prize laureate and the author of *Night* (about his experiences at Auschwitz concentration camp), was describing when he wrote, "Ultimately, the only power to which man should aspire is that which he exercises over himself."

Being *the greatness that you truly are* is about right here, right now. It occurs in the moment you choose to be all that is possible. When you are willing to embody and be the greatness you truly are, you are willing to create a life that goes beyond the limitations of what the rest of the world thinks is important. It is being willing to go beyond anything you have decided is you. This is not an easy task for most people, yet it's extremely crucial for achieving success in whatever you do! It's necessary for channelling your choices and energy in the most creative manner possible.

Function from possibilities.

I have personally discovered that conscious leadership is about allowing our inner leadership qualities to come forth. This requires us to live in the world as the greatness we are. This comes about when we choose to become more than what we have been willing to be.

Too often we are limited in what we can achieve in life because we haven't been willing to be more, to generate more, and to create more. We haven't been willing to function from possibilities. Clearly, then, expressing inner leadership qualities requires that we trust ourselves and honor who and what we are. Trusting and honoring ourselves is about the willingness to recognize what is true for us and *be that*—to be self-directed rather than directed by others in both our work and our life.

In sum, we all have the choice and the means within us to free ourselves from the constraints of this reality, which coerce us into imposed outlooks and responsibility. By choosing to become more than what we have been willing to be, we can create and generate a sustainable future unfettered by the limitations of this reality. We have a choice in life. Our choice creates our reality. By choosing to believe in our own abilities and challenge assumptions regardless of what conventional wisdom holds, we are on the way to being a conscious leader.

Choosing to be a conscious leader is the primary means for exercising our autonomy. By being willing to do whatever it takes to be this, we can shape our life, rather than be shaped by it. It's a continuous choice, moment by moment. Choice is an ongoing flow of energy that interacts with the world—continuously. Becoming greater than what we've been willing to be doesn't occur with just one choice. It occurs choice after choice after choice, which cumulatively change how we show up in the world.

Start living your life from this perspective: *What possibility could I choose here that would create something greater than I have ever been able to create before? What is possible that I have never even considered?* The impacts of these questions are profound. You will know that you have power to change anything in your life, to be something greater than you have ever been, if you choose.

Through choosing to be a conscious leader we no longer function unconsciously on autopilot but rather lead our own lives. Every choice we make in life creates different sets of possibilities, circumstances, and probabilities. So we have the infinite (limitless) choice of creating our life. Ultimately, when we acknowledge that there is a different possibility and a different consciousness that we can be if we choose it, we recognize that we absolutely have infinite choice with no limitation. It's self-evident that if the first choice we make doesn't work, all we have to do is just make a different choice. Infinite choice is the ability to choose it all.

The essence of having infinite choice is not the possession of some special power. It is much more the ability to choose. As long as you recognize that you are the source of creation, then you have infinite choice. If nothing is significant for you, then you always have infinite choice.

It comes from the willingness to lead a life without limitation. It is the willingness to be an energy that cannot be confined, defined, or limited. Nothing and no one stops you, and you don't need to stop or limit anyone else. If you function as anything less than that, you are choosing to be less than who and what you can be. There is a completely different reality available to you if you are willing to choose to be the greatness that you truly are.

I have been asked often to talk about what it means to embody and be the greatness of who we truly are. Many people misapply and misidentify being the greatness as being arrogant, egotistical, and self-important. This is not true. There's nothing lofty about it. It has nothing to do with self-important concepts.

To be the greatness of you is to be your own author and creator of your life. To discover your own innate powers and gifts, and then to find your own way to use them to create greater. It requires continuously choosing to be the possibility of something greater, something beyond what you have yet been willing to be. It's about truly being everything you are, regardless of anybody else's reality. You don't have to prove anything to anybody. There's no pretense, no illusion. When you've chosen to be the greatness of you, you are no longer putting on an act simply to fit in to the image posited by this reality.

The ability to create expands when you are willing to receive *the greatness you truly are*. It is not about doing; it is about being.

FOUR

To Become a Truly Conscious Leader, You Must Start with Yourself

Becoming a conscious leader in business, generating a sustainable future, and creating valuable products and services first and foremost requires you to commit to lead yourself and your own life.

For most people, choosing to become a leader is not a priority or an option. We are taught to study hard and work hard, to be normal, average, and fit in. We are taught to give up our awareness in order to buy the rightness of this reality. But who teaches us to totally value and trust ourselves? Who teaches us to honor who and what we are? Who teaches us to generate our life with ease? Who teaches us to generate money and wealth beyond the scope of work?

Most people think that you are born with the capacity to lead your own life, that you are born without it, or that your conditions and upbringing prime you. What if there is a different way of looking at the world? What if the very priority of your existence is to become aware of your own essential gifts—to acknowledge the greatness that you truly can be and express that in your daily activities?

Be a conscious leader of your life.

From working with a lot of leaders around the world, I know it is truly possible for people to cultivate the ability to lead their own lives. I have been helping leaders do it for over a decade. Cultivating this capacity requires you to make a commitment to living a life without limitation and give up habitual patterns of behavior that create tremendous limitation in your reality. You have to get to the awareness, "I'm not actually being a leader of my life, and I'm not really creating my life."

Not everyone can be a top chief executive and a leader of a major organization, but anyone can be a conscious leader of his or her own life. Choosing to be a conscious leader of your life is something that you can do every day. Being a conscious leader of your own life is being aware and recognizing that you are the generator for everything in your life. You are willing to be the leader and go where you are going, whether anybody else goes along or not. When you commit to be a leader of your life, you function from the space of what would create the greatest future possibilities. That's being the energy of creating beyond this reality. What would you create if you were being a conscious leader of your own life?

You can make a full commitment anytime you choose. The question is, do you make a full commitment to you and to actually being a leader of your life? Committing to being a leader of your life comes from within; it's everything you are and that you will be. It begins with a choice that leads to a series of external behaviors and actions. Sure, you can put on an image, a pretense, or a facade for people to look at.

But these things lack the energy that allows you to be the greatness that you can be. When you merely present an image of who you want people to see, you create an illusion. This false picture is a pretense of who you are. The ability to create different possibilities weakens when you go to an image. People swiftly spot phonies and pretenders. Your energy and who you choose to be as a person communicates more dynamically and accurately than the image you present.

What could be more generative, exciting, and full of possibilities than choosing to be the creator source of your own life? Of course, it is one thing to recognize the wisdom in an idea such as this. It is entirely another thing to really actualize it as your reality. A magnificent example is Coco Chanel.

When I think of people who have truly made a choice to be the creator source of their own life, who have actualized it and made it on their own, who have stood up for what they believe in, who have made a remarkable change when one was needed, Coco Chanel comes to mind. Coco Chanel completely redesigned the way women dressed during the 20th century.

In the 1920s, women dressed unadventurously, reflecting how they were still thought to be less than men. It was Coco Chanel who took unconventional ideas of fashion and ran with them. She was an innovator in many aspects of fashion. She developed a new kind of jewelry that imitated much more expensive jewelry. She launched her first perfume, Chanel No. 5, which was the first to feature a designer's name. She was critically acclaimed for her women's business suits, which turned the fashion industry upside down by converting clothing designed for males into female fashion.

Coco Chanel prided herself on her style and practicality combined with an awareness of what women wanted. It was this that made her the most memorable name in world fashion. She was willing to be controversial and to create fashion for women no one else had dared to try.

With her trademark suits and little black dresses, Chanel created timeless designs that are still admired today. She took her dreams, turned them into reality, and released women from their conventional attire.

Coco Chanel was willing to embody and be the greatness that she could truly be, willing to follow her knowing and be controversial. She wasn't afraid of failing. She didn't create her business by other people's points of view. She was not concerned about what people thought of her or her creations, or if her styles would be accepted, which showed in her inventive and generative designs.

Chanel showed women that they had a freedom of expression through their clothes and that they didn't need to be limited to the way others thought they should look. She showed that the only limit that exists is the one you have chosen to entertain within you.

If you really want to grow and expand beyond where you are today, you have to change the way you look at things. There doesn't have to be a limitation unless you choose it.

What was going on?

Back in the early 1990s, I was a senior executive of a Fortune 500 company. A blazing question I couldn't ignore arose from a trend that was happening regularly with business leaders. It didn't make sense to me: I saw that many extremely successful businesspeople were often unable to lead people well. They were known as strong leaders because of their ability to get results, but many were unfulfilled in their work and their personal lives. Even more puzzling, the leaders suffering this quandary seemed to be doing all the right things—fulfilling their strategy, increasing profits, and achieving success. They were earnestly following what they were taught in business school and at leadership trainings.

I was perplexed, in particular, about why these established leaders were unfulfilled not only by their work but also in their personal lives. There were growing incidents of executive derailment, where executives engaged in behaviors that caused harm to themselves and their organizations. What was going on? I knew the issue could not be due to leaders being unskilled or unqualified.

What I discovered was that while most of the leaders had strong management capacities, technical skills, knowledge, and education to conduct a successful business, they were inclined to not commit to leading their own life. They did not choose to be the conscious leader of their own life. Many leaders had not developed key skills that they needed to consciously lead their own life.

Despite the importance of being the leader of our own life, few people seem to possess this skill. Most of us aren't taught about the imperative of being the leader of our own life; instead, we get indoctrinated into cutting off our awareness in order to live in this reality. We have been conditioned to accept the notion that being normal, average, and regular, just like everybody else, is the best—even the *only*—way to be. We limit our awareness so we can fit in. We concentrate on not losing. Our entire upbringing has been about how to be in context with this reality. When we try to be in context with this reality, we have to judge every choice we make to ensure it is the right choice and won't have bad consequences.

So many people are merely surviving and so many business superstars wind up derailed. We cannot become a conscious leader in the world until we first become a conscious leader of our own life. This is exemplified by the well-known quote from Mahatma Gandhi: "Be the change you wish to see in the world." As we cultivate our innate ability to be the change we wish to see in the world, we see that we may have been turning away from infinite choices and infinite possibilities that we had the power and capacity to acknowledge, claim, and own. Turning away often means not recognizing how we may be creating paucity, smallness, and neediness as our reality. Do you get how much unconsciousness is attached to this way of being?

Create a reality that has more possibility in it.

Cultivating your innate ability to be the change you wish to see in the world begins with making a choice to be a conscious leader of your own life. You have to commit to you before you can lead your own life and become a conscious leader that others are inspired by. The Greek philosopher Socrates said it well: "To move the world we must first move ourselves."

When consciousness guides your priorities, vision, and practices, the result can be exceedingly affirmative. Conscious leaders can be the element that helps steer away from difficulties and toward infinite possibilities.

———

Consciousness is the ability to be present in your life in every moment, without judgment of you or anyone else. It is the ability to receive everything, reject nothing, and create everything you desire in life—greater than what you currently have, and more than what you can imagine.

—GARY DOUGLAS

———

In our work with countless organizations around the world, we have discovered that the consciousness of leaders has a profound effect on the ability of an organization to perform effectively. We have also observed that conscious leaders are able to create a thriving business when they choose to embody and be the conscious leader of their own life.

Over and over again, I have observed that when business executives do not take the important step leading themselves and their own life, they can be blinded by their limitations. Conversely, by becoming more conscious and aware in their personal self-leadership, not only do they gain greater insight about themselves, they are also able to create reality that has more possibility in it.

One of the most startling differences between people who choose to be a conscious leader of their own life and others is that they choose to create their life from the space of possibility rather than conclusion.

When we talk about being a conscious leader of our own life, we are talking about a state of being—not an action, not some meaningless charade. It's a generative energy, space, and consciousness. Being a conscious leader of your own life is something you choose. It is a choice you make. Consciousness is always a choice, just as anti-consciousness or unconsciousness is always a choice. It's never just a given. It's a choice in every moment of every day.

Open the doors to everything you are capable of.

In my view, Gary Douglas, founder of Access Consciousness, is one of the most benevolent conscious leaders of our time. It's been more than a decade since I first met Gary at the Mind, Body and Spirit symposium in Sydney, Australia. I had been a senior executive of a major corporation in Australia for 15 years and was very successful at my job. I had been conditioned to conform—to be logical, consistent, accountable, and buttoned up. I had a powerful desire to fit in and a strong need to remain in good standing with the group. I had been a good corporate citizen; I worked hard and lived up to my obligation. But being super successful according to this reality and other people's points of view and standards was not making me joyful.

During our conversation about consciousness and business, Gary said most people don't give themselves a place where they can be or do different. They take on fictitious or erroneous points of view about what they're supposed to be, what they're supposed to do, how something is supposed to be, or what's supposed to happen. They tend to cut off their awareness in order to conform to this reality.

When Gary was talking about people cutting off their awareness in order to conform, I was thinking, "Why would anyone choose that?" Then I became aware that *I* had been doing it. One thing that struck me intensely was the fact that I also had the need to conform, to fit in, to be like everybody else. The simple fact of the matter was that my conceivable universe belonged to other people's reality since I had been trying to create my reality from the rightness of somebody else's point of view.

It now seems crazy to me that I allowed myself to accept the notion that being unique and different was an impediment, while being normal, just like everybody else, was the best and only way to be. In an attempt to become a good corporate leader, I accepted faulty assumptions of how a leader should be. In fact, I'd worked myself up to be a fine corporate leader and conformed to the notion of being a great corporate citizen. The greater the desire to succeed the more we focus on fitting in and being the best according to this reality's point of view. But the desire to fit in and to conform can rob us of our joy of being.

Gary sparked my curiosity when he talked about the essentials of being the leader of your own life. My curiosity was ignited when he told me, "When you choose to become the leader of your own life, you open the doors to everything you are capable of, and all it takes is making a commitment to your life . . . This is so powerful that when you do it, you become part of creating a future where the entire universe can help." From this conversation, I realized that Gary had a power most people did not have, and I wanted to have that power.

Many people refuse this power, discard it, or just stay away from it. Some even negate and condemn it. Instead of ignoring the message or rejecting the power by trying to see a logical explanation of how it worked, I became fascinated. It was my curiosity and my wish to develop this power and possibility that set me off on a lifelong quest to fully embody and be the conscious leader of my own life.

Gary told me, "Being a conscious leader of your own life is about being everything you are, to live as you and be all of you, no matter what that turns out to be. It's about the energy you have to be." And he has lived by this maxim. Gary is willing to be the leader and go where he is going, whether anybody else goes along or not. He doesn't create his life according to somebody else's point of view. His choices aren't based on what is right or wrong according to this reality. They are based on what will create the most consciousness.

Gary chooses to embody consciousness in everything he does. This inspires me and many others to choose to become more conscious. He's committed to his life, to his awareness, and to consciousness. He is willing to recognize what is true for him and to be that, whether anybody else goes for it or not. Gary is always asking, "How will this create more consciousness?" As a result, his life keeps getting better and better and better. Who he is choosing to be encouraged me to question everything I thought was true. His way of being affirmed that being successful personally and being a contribution and a catalyst for different possibilities were not mutually exclusive.

"How can I fully embody and be the greatness that I truly am?" That's a question I still ask myself, especially when contemplating what I would like to create and what's next in my life. I've always considered myself as a seeker. And by that, I mean seeking to lead a life without limitation, to discover and acknowledge what is true for me and to be that, whether anybody else approves of me or not. Gary says, "You are the source for

creating the change you desire. But you have to be willing to be it! . . . Your being conscious actualizes a different reality. You become a catalyst for change." To truly be a catalyst for change and for different possibilities is my heart's unequivocal ultimate desire.

Create your own reality.

Businesses are full of anti-conscious leaders—people who have assumed that power comes from authority, control, and force. These people are inflexible in their attitudes, typically autocratic, and fear-driven. They attempt to control everything. I became aware of how I had been creating and controlling my reality according to my boss's reality and how I kept going back to the same old thing again and again. If we allow it, other people's points of view can completely immobilize us. And once these points of view that we bought as real have us under control, they strongly try to keep us from ever becoming the leader of our own life.

I became aware of when and how I allowed myself to be programmed this way. During an annual performance review many years ago, my boss, who epitomized the British "stiff upper lip" (with rigorous adherence to the protocols of conformity), encouraged me to see that being different was wrong. He gave me 10 out of 10 for my work performance but condemned me for being different, for thinking different, for sounding different. He told me that I needed to stop being different; I must conform and be more contextual if I wanted to climb any corporate ladder. From that moment, I completely bought into his point of view and gave up my awareness in order to buy the rightness of his reality. How silly was I to choose to do what someone else said was right for me and not to choose to be me, to be all of me?

Like me, you may have bought others' points of view that encouraged you to deem yourself unworthy. I know, without a doubt, that once you recognize these erroneous points of view you are able to let these false and fictitious programs go. It's not about undoing things. It's about recognizing, "This nonsensical program has been part of my reality." Once I recognized that I had been choosing other people's points of view as real, then it was up to me to be and do something different. I began to ask myself, "Do I wish to have this as my reality any longer?" I got a big "NO, NO, and unequivocally NO" for an answer.

I got to the point where I declared, no matter what it took, I was going to change me. I made a commitment to myself not to live by anyone else's judgment and reality ever again, no matter what. I was willing to commit to me, regardless of anything. Gary often says, "The one thing you can always change is you . . . All you can do is be and do something different to change you . . . What if you never had to be what other people wanted you to be? What if you only had to be what you wanted to be? It's called creating your own reality."

Making a bold choice to never live by anyone else's judgment and reality ever again was the only way to advance toward becoming a conscious leader of my own life. This was a CHOICE I was willing to make. I told myself, "No matter what it takes, no matter what it looks like, if I lose everybody I know and everything I hold valuable in this reality, I am going down this path."

This choice gave (and gives) me access to a whole new way of being. I realized that I had nothing but myself to work with. I began by acknowledging that no one except me could teach me how to create my own reality, to take charge, or to be committed to myself. I realized the only thing I have total authority over is myself, my viewpoint, and my own reality.

Making a 100 percent commitment to myself meant that I would be and do everything possible to create my own reality and to never live by anyone else's judgment and reality ever again. It meant taking charge of my future and creating it the way I desired it to be, rather than just being on autopilot mode and wishing for a great outcome.

I made a commitment to myself: "I'm going to do and be whatever it takes for this to no longer be part of my reality." I had to keep reminding myself that other people's beliefs and judgments have no power. Instead, it is my point of view about other people's beliefs and judgments that have the power.

Every time a judgment comes up, I say to myself, "Interesting point of view that I have this point of view," otherwise it relentlessly comes back. The moment that it appears, I say, "Okay, I'm buying an erroneous viewpoint again. I would choose this for what reason?" When I say, "Interesting point of view that I have this point of view," I don't become involved in other people's opinions or beliefs. I don't become the effect of them. It's just allowance for what is.

Developing the ability to see every point of view as just an interesting point of view allows me to flow with the moment. I experience less stress and emotional turbulence. Ultimate freedom lies in the awareness that a point of view is not right or wrong, good or bad. It's just an interesting point of view. When I function with that allowance, there's no way anybody else can own me.

Total choice and total possibility.

When we summon the courage to *choose* to lead a life without limitation, when we dare to be different, when we dare to change ourselves or even simply do something outside of what others call the norm, we become a true conscious leader of our own life. And it is a very different place to function from.

Gary asks, "What if you were never right? What if you were never wrong? . . . What if everything you ever thought was a wrongness about you was a power and potency? What if your difference is the possibility, not the wrongness?" These questions have been my salvation. I began to look more closely at the things my boss judged as wrong about me when he told me that being different was a wrongness. I then asked, "Is this something wrong or is this something *strong* I have not been willing to acknowledge?" This question allowed me to recognize the strengths I had not been acknowledging.

So, why are these questions relevant to becoming a conscious leader of your own life? Because your power and potency come from the awareness of the difference you are. Whether you ever thought there was a wrongness about you or not, you can benefit from the gift that these questions provide. That gift is the key to different possibilities. *When you have no judgment or point of view about you, you have truly claimed and owned your power and potency.*

———

What if you start to trust the one person you have never trusted before . . . you! . . . What if you were willing to nurture and care for you? What if you would open the doors to being everything you have decided it is not possible to be? What would it take for you to realize how crucial you are to the possibilities of the world?

—GARY DOUGLAS

———

When you live your life by somebody else's reality, nothing that does not match their reality can even come into your awareness. As a result, you don't have total choice. Living your life by your reality and not somebody else's is the point where you recognize your capacity for choice—a powerful choice that gives you power, potency, and action, putting you in control and not at the effect of anybody. It's the place where you have true choice.

Real progress in life requires you to create without conclusion. The key is to ask, "If there was no conclusion about what I was choosing, what would I create?" You have to get to the place where you are willing to have total choice and total possibility—with no point of view about how it shows up or what it looks like when it does show up. It's not about getting it the way you want. It's not about completion; it's about awareness. It's about being aware and recognizing that you are the generator for everything in your life.

What possibilities do you see in yourself? Imagine what you could achieve in your life and business if you lived by your reality and not by somebody else's reality. A person who is a true conscious leader knows what works for them. Whether anybody else gets it or not is irrelevant. A conscious leader chooses to be everything they are, regardless of whether anybody else goes along with it. They have total choice because they are willing to be aware. In fact, they are willing to be never right, never wrong, and always aware.

You will never see the wrongness of you when nothing is right, nothing is wrong, and everything is just a choice. With total choice, you can create anything, and all things become possible. When you don't judge what's right or wrong, every choice you make and every action you take can lead to new possibility. What if you adopted the mindset that there was no such thing as right or wrong, good or bad? What possibility do you have here that you have never considered? Imagine where you could take your career if you were willing to have total choice and total possibility.

Commit to something way larger
than your own life.

When we are immersed in creating a business and generating money, we inadvertently become contextual, materialistic, impulsive, brash, or controlling. We unconsciously get caught up in our fears of not having enough. We become disengaged from our awareness in order to "get what's ours" or incessantly trying to "get more."

If you're a leader of a business, you're sculpting the energy of your business even when you don't deliberately set out to do it. Much of leadership is the way you live, the way you speak, the way you think, the way you behave, the way you relate to people, the way you operate your business, the daily choices you make. Most important, leadership is who you are choosing to be. To be a conscious leader is to have generative energy, space, and consciousness with all aspects of your life. When you're having a terrible day and don't feel like leading, you're leading others to have a bad day. When you're a leader, you cannot *not* lead. You're modeling all the time.

In my view, conscious leaders are truly committed to something way larger than their own life, way larger than their own business. They are committed to generating greater possibilities and having vision greater than they can imagine—even greater than what they can accomplish in their lifetime. Gandhi, Eleanor Roosevelt, Coco Chanel, Martin Luther King, Jr., Nelson Mandela, J. K. Rowling, Marie Curie . . . the list goes on of people we truly admire who have chosen to create something larger than their own life. Their life is a contribution to that continuum.

FIVE

Pragmatic Choice

Choosing to be the leader of your own life is fundamental to the work of a business leader, and it is the first requirement of conscious leadership. From that quality springs all generative energy, space, and consciousness that allows you to claim, own, and acknowledge who and what you are.

When I spent time with Gary Douglas, I realized that he saw a completely different reality. He chooses to make his life about infinite possibilities and infinite choice. He functions from pragmatic choice, which means he follows the energy, follows his knowing, and deals with what is—with fact and what is going on, rather than from conclusion, assumption, projection, expectation, or judgment. If everybody chooses to live this way, we'd transform the world.

Access Consciousness shows that it is truly possible to create a thriving business with conscious awareness. Founded by Gary in 1995, Access is a worldwide movement. It is about facilitating consciousness and awareness and knowing. The target is empowering people to access what they know—not to tell them what to do. Gary describes it as an applied philosophy for life. A key difference of Access from other philosophies, however, is that it is organic, constantly changing, and invites contribution from everyone who participates in it.

At every turn, Access has taken the road less traveled. For over two decades, Gary has generated and instituted new approaches to business that inspired people to see the world through different eyes and lead their lives with conscious awareness. Five years ago, Access Consciousness was in 40 countries; today it's more than 170. Gary's accomplishments demonstrate, beyond a doubt, the efficacy to leading with conscious awareness.

The key difference between traditional business leaders and Gary is that traditional business leaders often seek to establish limits. Gary looks beyond them. He is not bound by rigid forms and structures that others have deemed highly important and significant. He follows his knowing rather than using force and effort as a way of making things occur in the business. He says, "When you function from the place of following your knowing instead of giving up what you know in favor of what somebody else says you should do, you will always know what is right for you."

Without any projection and expectation or conclusion and as-sumption, the ability to follow the energy and follow your knowing is always available. To generate sustainable futures, leaders must have an awareness of what they would like to generate in the world energeti-cally and carry the awareness of that energy with them no matter where they go and no matter what they do.

What makes Gary so notable is that he has created a fusion of consciousness, benevolence, and capitalism—a new system and a dif-ferent approach for creating and generating business. Gary is able to generate an unorthodox business because he doesn't let the controls of other people's points of view, realities, judgments, and decisions be the controlling factor in his life: "When I first started doing Access, it's like I had all kinds of people who were always trying to tell me you can't do it that way. And I would look at them and go to myself: Can I do it this way? Not that they're right or they're wrong. But, well, can I do it this way? And will it work for me? And I always got a yes. So, I followed my knowing and I did what I did the way I knew it would work and it always worked. Why? Because I'm the only one who has all the information about what's going to make my business work."

Gary leads the business by allowing Access to be in a constant state of creating itself new, moment to moment, instead of maintaining its identity. He is not defined by other people's expectations and beliefs about what he should be. Gary is an outstanding demonstration of a conscious leader that has achieved phenomenal success and is also making a positive contribution to society and the world. He has created space for greater possibilities by establishing clear leadership and governance, and integrating conscious and benevolent (wishing well for all) business practices across all of his business operations. Access Consciousness has created a number of programs and initiatives that are currently in place or part of the future strategy. This is a very different paradigm for creating and generating a totally different reality.

Every time you choose from a conscious place by following your knowing, you generate a plethora of possibilities. Every time you go against your knowing, you kill every possibility that you could generate for your business. Because Gary is willing to follow what he knows, he's aware when something isn't working before it doesn't work, not after it's not working.

Gary has always been present with what is and totally aware of what can and can't be. He doesn't look for something to be greater than what is. He always makes his choice from awareness, never from conclusion or the rightness of somebody else's point of view. He is willing to find what works for him. He asks questions like, "What do I need to be aware of here? Where is everyone functioning from? What is going to be generative for my business and for me in my life?" Questions allow him to have awareness of the big picture and awareness of the situation at hand. He has an astounding capacity for eliminating any preconceptions and seeing things through a fresh, unfiltered lens. This allows him to see the situation accurately and open-mindedly.

Most of us are not able to see different possibilities with ease because we tend to get bogged down by following norms and aligning our business with conventional business models. When my husband and I started our consultancy business two decades ago, we created our business structure around conventional principles; we followed the norm and aligned ourselves with conventional business models, all in an endeavor to achieve good outcomes. For example, we often perceived that we shouldn't take up a particular project, but we ignored our perceptions because the traditional models showed we should do the project. We knew it was going to turn out badly, yet we did it anyway. Most of the time they turned out just as badly as we knew they would.

We became aware that for us to thrive and meet the challenges of the hyper-changing environment, we had to stop following conventional business models and instead truly begin to follow our knowing. This is about being willing to receive the information that is available. It involves asking questions so that our awareness has an avenue for responding. We asked questions, followed the energy, and made conscious choices based on the information and awareness we perceived and received. Our global businesses are testaments to power of those choices.

The essence of pragmatic choice is not the possession of some superior capacity; it is much more that ability to be the question. Here are the kind of questions we use to get us into the space to be aware of different possibilities: What's possible here? What choices do I have? What do I need to be aware of today? Is there some place I need to put my energy or my attention today?

When we follow our knowing, we are aware whether our choice will be expansive and create more possibilities or whether it will be contractive and create limitation for us and everyone else. This greatly enhances the probability of our success. We began to truly function from pragmatic choice at the moment when we make a conscious choice to follow our knowing.

Pragmatic choice is a truly indispensable power of conscious leadership. It also provides practical support for everyday life. The Japanese have a word for this approach: *arugamama*. It means the virtue of abiding with things as they are. It implies a pragmatic choice and pragmatic approach to life. Very often, business leaders have frustration with business and a general despondency in life. The problem is, what they experience is in contrast to life as they project or expect or imagine it should be. They have made a judgment, "Life is not the way that it should be." So, they strive to make life more closely match their projections and expectations. The consequence is that they function in a kind of constant judgment and frustration with what is emerging, expecting that once they fix what they believe is wrong they will be fulfilled. This might seem to be a perfectly reasonable formula for personal development, but there are some serious downsides to trying to make life match your projections.

Every choice creates a new set of possibilities.

The most important understanding we can have about choice is that every choice we make in life creates. One more time: every choice we make in life creates. Every choice creates different sets of possibilities, different sets of circumstances, different sets of probabilities. You have the choice of creating your life. Choice creates.

Every choice creates a change, and every choice creates a new set of possibilities. You have to choose in order to have the awareness of what your choice creates. If you're not happy with your creation, make a new choice, a different choice. Every choice creates a change, and every choice creates a new set of possibilities. If you will acknowledge what is, then you can have other choices as well.

My personal life has been enriched and enhanced by applying pragmatic choice and cultivating the capacity to be present with what is. And because of that, reality continually presents itself as a fresh moment. The more I function from pragmatic choice, the more possibilities I have in my life. This tool gives me a way to generate a delightful life and a thriving business—both with my husband. The skill of pragmatic choice allows us to work together toward a thriving business and still have fun being and living with each other every day.

Since the early 2000s, Steve and I have joyfully and dynamically created our consultancy business to help CEOs and leadership teams become conscious leaders and raise their levels of awareness so they can have an even greater impact. Functioning from pragmatic choice allows us to always be on a create cycle, not a maintenance cycle. This way of being allows us to be on a generative edge of different possibilities.

We have seen too many people destroy their business and their relationships because they just wanted to maintain instead of creating. For Steve and me, to create our relationship on a create cycle rather than a maintenance cycle we choose to destroy and uncreate everything our relationship was yesterday. We start new every day. To free ourselves from habit, to resolve conflicts, to transcend our fixed points of view, we start each day brand-new with no judgments carried forward.

This tool allows us to be in a constant state of generating and creating our relationship instead of creating from old points of view.

Likewise, we chose to create our business in perpetual motion, traveling globally, working with business leaders of large and small companies, and running workshops around the world. We have made a conscious choice to create our life and our business from possibilities, choice, question, and the contribution we can be and receive. Every day is a new possibility for our relationship and our business, not based on any old points of view.

The skill of pragmatic choice includes being able to trust our awareness, our knowing, and our perception. Trusting these things shows us in a flash the different possibilities that would create something beyond what we have considered. Pragmatic means choosing what works—always. Everyone has this capacity; we just have to learn to trust it. Most people try to justify *why* they're choosing what they're choosing. I never justify what I choose; I choose what I know is possible. Please recognize that you don't *have* to have a reason for anything you choose.

Pragmatic choice is rooted in knowing that I will always have access to infinite choice and infinite possibilities. This capacity to function from pragmatic choice has given me the power to transform my businesses and my investment portfolios into multiple streams of possibilities beyond the limitations of this reality.

Is pragmatic choice a skill that can be learned? You bet. To do this, you have to expand your ability to perceive all that is happening around you without buying thoughts, biases, and feelings as real. Simply trust your knowing. In fact, if you make it a practice to follow your knowing as you go about your daily life, even with the small stuff, you will move toward that which expands your life and possibilities.

Choice is just choice. You can choose again and again and again.

There is always a moment where you can make a different choice. Pragmatic choice invites us to lighten up, look around, and recognize that there is no wrong choice. It offers an alternative to the controlling way many of us try to lead our lives. Every choice you make creates awareness and determines what your future can be. So, when you make a choice, recognize what possibilities or limitations are being generated with that choice.

Most of us have been taught to choose based on making a *right* choice. Which means we have to figure out what is the right choice. We try to figure it out logically to make sure that nothing will go wrong if we finally make this choice. The need to make the right choice increases the tendency to rely on known patterns—what we know to be secure and conservative choices. When we have a need to choose the *right* choice above all else, it becomes harder, even impossible, to take risks.

You have infinite choice and infinite possibilities!

Conscious leaders recognize that choice is never right or wrong or good or bad. Every choice creates. Every choice is greater possibility. And every time you choose you are creating something. Gary teaches that when you are willing to perceive everything without judgment, you have infinite choice. The more I perceive things as they are, without any judgment or attempt to define them, the greater my awareness of what's occurring in the world.

Of course, there are many factors that can shift the market and the industry that may affect your business. The less perception you have the more easily you will be swept along by the forces of conventional reality and the less generative you will be in your life and business. The greater your perception the more aware you are of future trends and how these trends may affect you and your business. You will perceive changes and opportunities and be more likely to recognize new and different possibilities. In fact, when you're willing to perceive everything, you are able to recognize and distinguish changes, positive and negative, that may affect your organization and the world.

A great example of this kind of perception comes from Muhammad Yunus, a Bangladeshi social entrepreneur, banker, economist, and civil society leader who was awarded the Nobel Peace Prize for founding the Grameen Bank and pioneering the concepts of microcredit and microfinance, especially for impoverished women. Yunus was willing to perceive the world through different eyes and was able to create far beyond what was considered possible.

On a field trip to the poor Bangladeshi village of Jobra, he discovered that the bamboo-weaving women of the village had to borrow money for raw materials, which left them almost nothing as a profit margin. He perceived there was a different possibility, especially if the women could borrow at lower rates. Following this perception—and without any judgment of how others might view this—he set about approaching banks to provide microloans. All turned him down. Yet he was still willing to perceive how the future might look if poor women were able to create their own entrepreneurial businesses. So, he funded the first microloans from his own pocket (the equivalent of US$27) to 42 basket weavers in the village. They paid him back on time. Then he did it again and again. He was willing to be and do anything to create a greater possibility.

Most people use money to create a result for themselves. They do a business in order to make profit. Muhammad Yunus recognized that money can be used to create a different reality. His Grameen Bank used money as a way of creating a different reality in the world. By following his perception, without any idea of how it should look, he created a new system for banking that fundamentally changed the world. Conventional reality said it could not work. His perception of what was possible and what needed to change led him to create a major financial and social system that was recognized by a Nobel Peace Prize.

In his words, "In creating Grameen Bank, I never had a blueprint to follow. I moved one step at a time, always thinking this step will be my last step. But it was not. That one step led me to another step, a step that looked so interesting that it was difficult to walk away from. I faced this situation at every turn." Muhammad Yunus is an amazing example of perceiving opportunities and changes, with no judgment based on this reality's expectations.

Choice is the way to navigate change

Choice is a remarkable way to navigate change when you function from the question, "What possibility could I choose here that would create something greater than I have ever been able to create before?" It is not about *seeing* the possibility. It is choosing *for* the possibility, even though you have no idea what it looks like. It's utterly different from reaching a conclusion about what something is or has to be.

When you choose *for* the possibility, you create from a different possibility and a different reality. The possibilities are based on the energy you can perceive, not on the vision you can receive. It doesn't require any justifications or reasons. Yunus has demonstrated what choosing *for* the possibility can achieve. When he followed his knowing, he made choices that most people would call ridiculous: He provided microfinancing for the poorest of the poor, the beggars, so they could sell small items like sweets and toys as well as beg. He provided phone loans to 100,000 "telephone ladies" in villages, who now act as the hub for village communications. His knowing led him to loan almost exclusively to women and only in small groups or borrowing circles. There was no economic model to follow, no past success from those before him. It was just his knowing that made this possible.

Choice is an ongoing flow of energy that interacts with the world continuously. There is no right or wrong or good or bad choice. It's just a choice. What you choose only gives you awareness, it does not give you a right or wrong or a consequence. You may be surprised to learn that choice is the beginning of all creation. Every choice creates a change and every choice creates a new set of possibilities. Every time you choose, something shows up in your life because of your choice. There's no right or wrong choice. There's just choice.

Function from pragmatic choice.

The fundamental skill of a conscious leader is the ability to be present with what is and the ability to be aware of what can and can't be. Gary says, "The reason most average people don't generate their business and their financial reality that is greater than the one they already have is that they are not being all the awareness they are. They are defined by other people's expectations and beliefs about what they should be. Most leaders let circumstances define their lives. Most people don't function in the moment from pragmatic choice, where they can deal with what is, where they can change anything as needed to accomplish and create more."

Functioning from pragmatic choice is about possibilities, choices, and awareness. When you create your life and business from this space, you have no investment in the outcome—and no idea of what might show up. There is only awareness of the energy. When you start to function from pragmatic choice, you look at fact, at what is transpiring, and you ask the questions, "How is this going to work? What is this going to lead to? What possibility do I have here?"

If you would like to function from pragmatic choice, simply start by asking questions: "What choice do I have now? What choice do I need to make here? What would I like to choose? What will this create? How is this going to create a future in which everything improves?"

If things are not working for you, say, "Okay, this isn't working. What do I need to change? What else needs to be different? What can I change today? Where can I put my energy that would change something?"

People who function from pragmatic choice are always being the question that would create a possibility. They are about opening to the choice of new possibility—to the question of what *can* get created instead of the conclusion of what *should* be created.

A great example of this is Sir Timothy John Berners-Lee, the British inventor. In 1989, Tim Berners-Lee came up with the idea that eventually became the World Wide Web. The World Wide Web started life in the CERN physics laboratory in Switzerland in the early 1990s. Initially, Berners-Lee's innovation was intended to help scientists share data across a then-obscure platform called the Internet, a version of which the U.S. government had been using since the 1960s. Owing to Berners-Lee's pragmatic choice to release the source code to make the Web an open and democratic platform for all, the Web quickly took on a life of its own.

At the same time that Berners-Lee introduced the Web to the world freely, competing technologies, such as Gopher, developed at the University of Minnesota in the United States, were also offering a way of connecting documents on the Internet for a price. But the World

Wide Web succeeded because Berners-Lee knew that for it to reach its full potential it would have to be freely available. He was choosing for the possibility, based on the energy he could perceive, not on conclusion, projection, or expectation according to this reality. He had it in mind that the Web should be a force for good. Yet he also perceived that it had infinite potential to develop in unimaginable directions.

Apart from his pioneering idea, what makes Berners-Lee extraordinarily special is his amazing capacity to function from pragmatic choice. Not all the bosses at CERN were in favor of making the Web universally accessible. Berners-Lee was able to go beyond looking at the potential and ask, "What are the possibilities that I have never even considered?" He didn't come to conclusions about anything. He was willing to see the reality he was in. He was willing to look at and ask, "What is it? How is it going to work? What is this going to look like? What is it going to lead to?"

Since the world knew nothing about the potential of the Web, most conventional strategic analysis would have pointed to limited potential for growth. Berners-Lee had to convince them that the Web was such an immense innovation that CERN couldn't hold on to it, and the best thing to do was to give it away. He persuaded his bosses to provide the program code for free. Since then, the Web has exploded into every area of life. According to recent figures offered by Internet World Stats, there are an estimated 1.133 billion people around the world engaging in regular use of the Internet. And with more than 165 million different destinations available through its virtual pages, the Internet has grown into a groundbreaking, and seemingly limitless, communications tool.

The key characteristic of pragmatic choice is flexibility.

Flexibility is the willingness and capacity to change and transform naturally and spontaneously as circumstances emerge. Over the coming decades, the flexibility of every leader and organization will be tested as never before.

Flexibility is what you need to take full advantage of the new and different possibilities created by being a conscious leader of your own life. Without flexibility, you'll be unable to handle the world as it changes constantly around you. You'll always be operating in the past—on old assumptions that you project into the future or worries about what might happen. The most dangerous path to business derailment comes from leaders who lack flexibility.

The leaders at Blockbuster, Kodak, Polaroid, Tower Records, and Borders, for example, were so fixed in their ways that they couldn't take advantage of the industry's early warning signals of massive impending change in their industry. They turned a blind eye toward the digital revolution. The experience of these organizations illustrates just how devastating it can be when leaders lack flexibility and choose to lead a company with rigid form and structure.

One of the best predictors of an organization's health is how well the leadership team adapts and responds to changes. In today's swiftly evolving and increasingly changeable world, organizations cannot afford to deploy leaders with fixed points of view. The degree to which leaders' function from fixed points of view is in direct proportion to their inability to innovate.

Great opportunities in business always come from occurrences and events that are happening now. If you are blinded by your fixed points of view, you won't see the opportunities until it's too late. In fact, you won't see anything that doesn't match your point of view. You've got to get to the place where you are willing to have total choice and total possibility—with no point of view about how it shows up or what it looks like when it shows up. *You must be willing to give up your fixed points of view.*

The full benefits of functioning from pragmatic choice come only to the person who approaches every moment with a deep sense of openness, without any fixed point of view. This is where you choose from possibility, where you create from possibility, and where you have infinite possibility.

SIX

Being Conscious Is About
the Everyday!

From the experiences I have created over the last 25 years, working with a wide range of people around the world, I can affirm that anyone can choose to be conscious and aware if they choose to claim, own, and be it. People are born with an innate capacity to be conscious and aware, but this capacity weakens and declines when we don't access it.

Awareness is not a supernatural power that only special people are blessed with. It's part of our innate capacity. We don't have to be in an altered state of consciousness to access it. Given the right tools and practices, all of us can cultivate our consciousness and open up to an expanded awareness of what is possible.

Being conscious is the state of being totally aware, totally present in all areas of your life. It is the ability to always be aware of more possibility, more choice, and more life. Being conscious is about the everyday. It has to do with awareness of everything that's possible. That's it. It is not about enlightenment or a supernatural mode of being or having magical powers.

Being a conscious leader starts with choosing to be conscious and aware of where you are, who you are choosing to be, and why you are doing what you are doing. This is vital! Many of us have trouble accepting this choice for ourselves, but that's something that remarkable leaders—Albert Einstein, Leonardo da Vinci, Socrates, Golda Meir, Martin Luther King, Jr., Eleanor Roosevelt, Steve Jobs, Gary Douglas, Richard Branson, Warren Buffett, Jonas Salk, Tim Berners-Lee, Peter Drucker, and so many others—do naturally.

Expand what is possible.

We all have capacity to choose to be conscious—to function from awareness and perceive wonder in every moment and every day—but we've been lulled into the unawareness of autopilot mode. Have you ever wondered what sets certain business leaders apart from the rest? They seem to achieve things with ease and effortlessness. What makes it possible for them to prosper and thrive while the rest of us watch in awe and wonder?

Different possibilities come to those who make a conscious choice to lead their life with conscious awareness. I don't want to live a numbed, shut-down, and unconscious life, desensitized to awareness of new and different possibilities. I choose every day to have a generative energy, space, and consciousness for expanding what is possible. To experience joy and infinite possibilities on every level.

You will find that a conscious life requires constant vigilance. It requires being committed to embracing conscious awareness as a way of being and allowing your inner leadership qualities to come forth. It is a commitment you make to yourself: to not live by anyone else's judgment and reality ever again, no matter what.

Embracing and being a conscious leader is about looking within to see what would expand your awareness and then following through on any and all activities that can generate different possibilities. This requires you to live in the world as the greatness you are, which then invites everyone else to be the greatness they are.

Be a catalyst for change.

Being a conscious leader is not about what you *have* to do; it's about making the choice to be a conscious leader. You begin to expand your consciousness at the moment when you choose for yourself to be conscious and to fully immerse yourself in being totally aware and totally present. When you choose to be a conscious leader, you become the catalyst for a different possibility in the world.

When business leaders really begin to choose to be and do everything from conscious awareness, that is when new and different possibilities begin to emerge in their business and in the world. For me, it is a pleasure to be a leader inspiring people to live and lead with conscious awareness. It is a delight to be a catalyst for other people to choose to be a conscious leader in their own life and in the world.

My primary target in life, my most essential priority, is to be a catalyst for change and for different possibilities in the world. And my number-one leadership and personal practice is choosing to be and to live in the present moment—to stop functioning from conclusion, projection, expectation, judgment, and assumption. I started with the premise that anything is changeable, and anything can be different if I am willing to choose it. Being a catalyst requires question, choice, possibility, and contribution. I started asking, "What is my priority? What choice do I have? What else is possible? What contribution can I be?" I was looking for an awareness; I wasn't looking for "why" or the answer.

Asking these questions allowed me to know my priority. When I got clear on what my priority was, I created it easily. I became aware that I had something to offer the world that I had not been willing to offer. It was the awareness of what else I could create in the world that I hadn't yet created. Once I recognized and acknowledged that my priority was to fully be the change that I would like to see in the world, I began to actively seize new and different possibilities. I chose to live in the question, what can I be or do different that would create and generate more for me and for everyone concerned? With this question, there was a new, real sense of what was possible.

I became aware that there was a different possibility. I was able to acknowledge what I could be, do, have, create, or generate that I have never before been, done, had, created, or generated as me. I was able to find the means to achieve my priority and act on the possibility of things. When I had this awareness of what I could create, all kinds of amazing things started showing up.

But again, it's not about trying to create an end result of some kind. Choosing to be a catalyst for change is a place of adventure for me—an ongoing creative and generative movement. It is about the moment when I know that what I've done will change something. Being a catalyst for change and for different possibilities is one of the most important qualities of conscious leadership.

Can you imagine what it would be like to do everything from the place of consciousness that invites the whole world to function with you, not against you? Conscious awareness expands the world. And when leaders are functioning consciously, they can become architects and catalysts for making the world a better place. They can contribute to the greater good because they are willing to be agents of change. They are capable of changing the world and transforming the people around them. These leaders stand in the great space of infinite possibility in a posture of openness, with an unrepressed imagination for what is possible. They are open to all possibility and sincerely willing to look at what they can do to generate different possibilities.

An example of a business leader who made the choice to be a catalyst for different possibilities is Jeffrey Skoll, a founder and chairman of the Skoll Foundation. A Canadian engineer, Internet entrepreneur, and film producer, with an estimated net worth of US$3.8 billion (as of September 2013), Skoll was ranked by *Forbes* as the 7th wealthiest Canadian and 347th in the world. Skoll set in motion a spirit of conscious leadership that nurtures the courage to break new ground and the boldness to go beyond limitations of this reality.

Skoll was aware of new and different possibilities. He was able to conceive new ideas and new strategies to bring those ideas into existence. He was the first employee and first president of eBay and used the wealth this gave him to become a philanthropist, particularly through the Skoll Foundation and the media company he founded, Participant Media.

Skoll is bringing life to his vision of a sustainable world of peace and prosperity. Over the last 15 years, he has created an innovative social enterprise: investing in a range of efforts that integrate powerful possibilities and data with entrepreneurial approaches. Participant Media funds feature films and documentaries that promote social values while still being commercially viable. The company has released 43 films and garnered 35 Oscar nominations, while contributing to social change. These films are now household names: *Wonder*, *The Cove*, *The Best Exotic Marigold Hotel*, *The Hundred-Foot Journey*, *Food, Inc.*, and *The Help*. What makes Skoll different is that he has created these films not from judgment but from a level of awareness that asks people to question what they think they know.

In 2009, Skoll created the Skoll Global Threats Fund, focused on responding quickly to events that threaten the world's health and stability. The foundation uses a variety of tools to tackle problems like climate change and conflict in the Middle East.

Conscious leadership is about right here, right now. It is the moment you choose to be all that is possible.

---

*Being conscious is never seeing being
conscious as separate from you*

No matter who we are or where we have come from, we all have an innate capacity to be conscious and aware. Still, this is a very new frontier for most people. Some people do not believe that consciousness is real. We are trained to disregard our consciousness, to ignore our awareness, to snub our knowing, and to abandon our ability to follow the energy. For many of us, the habit is so ingrained that we don't notice we are doing it.

When I made a conscious choice to adopt the conscious leadership way of being, it began with a choice—a simple choice that I made to be the leader of my own reality, no matter what. When I began to fully immerse myself in being totally aware, totally present, everything I was being and doing became the source of everything that would create different possibilities in my business and my life. Now, every time I turn a corner, something new shows up.

When I committed to becoming a conscious leader of my own life, I began to realize what I am and what I could be. I began to see that I could create me as the gift, me as the possibility, and me as the inspiration for a different reality. Being a conscious leader is where I choose from possibility, where I create from possibility, and where I have infinite possibility.

When you choose to function from conscious awareness, this becomes who you are in the world. If you are not willing to be conscious, you can't have it; if you're not willing to have it, you can't be it. When you make a choice to step into being a conscious leader, you simply become that energy and the vibration that will allow it to come to you. It cannot show up in your life if you're not being it.

Most of us don't realize how much our consciousness influences other people's behavior. Many of us are oblivious to how obstructive and disruptive our unconsciousness and anti-consciousness can be. Conversely, there's no denying that a business leader in the midst of functioning and leading with conscious awareness is spectacularly present. These leaders carry a palpable, generative energy.

This vibrational energy, commonly known as magnetism or harmonic coherence frequency, strongly affects others around you. When you expand your awareness and immerse yourself in being totally aware and totally present, you create a stirring of energy throughout your surroundings and your organization. You create a different possibility with every person you talk to.

SEVEN

What Does It Mean to Be a Catalyst?

A catalyst is a substance that when added to or mixed with another component accelerates a change in it without altering itself. It's a person or thing that acts as a stimulus in bringing about a result.

All of us have a catalytic capacity—if we choose to claim, own, and acknowledge it. It is not a mystical power that only a chosen few are blessed enough to be born with. It is a natural ability that can be developed by anyone. It is an innate capability that everyone possesses but very few choose to cultivate. It has been covered up by a whole lot of self-imposed limitations for a long time.

When you are a catalyst for change, the energy and awareness you bring to a situation allows change to occur. As Gary puts it, "You have a catalytic capacity. Literally, by the questions you ask, the things you do and say, you can transform and change people around you. The willingness to be present and aware, to be in allowance, is a potency that can change anything."

Have you ever seen someone completely change the energy of all the people in a room, simply by walking into it? When you are truly being a conscious leader, you have the potency to change the world and the people around you with the energy you *are*. As a leader, if you walk into a room full of crisis, turmoil, dispute, and confusion, you can change the energy from problem to possibilities by virtue of the catalytic energy you *are*—if you are willing to be this. That is the potency of life: the ability to be the catalyst for change and transformation of all things and everyone. You have to be willing to be so potent that nothing stops the consciousness you are.

Energetic entrainment frequency.

This vibration of a catalyst affects others in a multitude of ways through a process known as entrainment. Entrainment can be defined as the tendency for two oscillating bodies to lock into phase so that they vibrate in harmony. This is called harmonic coherence.

Entrainment is a recognized law that affects the natural world. The principle of entrainment is universal and has been scientifically validated in a vast number of areas of study, including astronomy, chemistry, pharmacology, biology, medicine, neurology, psychology, sociology, music, architecture, and many other disciplines. Scientists have observed the law of entrainment in heart cells placed near each other. They have noted it in speech and body patterns in human dialogue. It also describes the way a group of musicians manages to play in time together. Entrainment can also be observed in all animal and plant species. A group of fireflies gathered in an area will flash at the same time. Flocks of birds in flight often flap their wings in unison. A huge amount of research has been done into entrainment in living things. Some researchers have stated that entrainment appears to be essential to life itself.

The history of entrainment is linked to findings of the Dutch scientist Christian Huygens (1629–1695). Huygens was a leading scientist of his time and the inventor of the pendulum clock. While working on the design of the pendulum clock, he found that when he placed two clocks on a wall near each other and swung the pendulums at different rates, they would eventually end up swinging at the same rate.

This also occurred when a room was filled with grandfather clocks of different sizes and pendulum lengths. Each pendulum was set swinging at a different rate, and after a period of time, the clocks became synchronized with each other by sending and receiving minute vibrations through the walls and floor of the building. Not only was energy being transferred, individual clocks altered their "behavior" in order to become synchronized with the other clocks. Equally noteworthy is the fact that the slower (lower frequency) clocks picked up their pace to become synchronized with the fastest (highest frequency) clock. This entrainment process has been replicated over and over through the centuries and has given rise to many scientific and arts-related disciplines.

The explanation for this phenomenon is that very small amounts of energy are transferred between the two objects when their vibrations or frequencies are not the same. The energy transfer forces the two objects to start vibrating at the same speed. The weaker system is entrained by the stronger system, so when two objects of like vibration are in close proximity, the object of lesser (weaker) vibration will begin to match the object of stronger vibration.

Recent scientific research in the fields of chaos theory and quantum mechanics has shown that everything and everyone in the universe, every thought and every attitude, gives off a vibration or a frequency, and that all things are connected through energy. We all are broadcasting stations radiating our energetic signals to the world. Each of us has a particular frequency or vibration—a consciousness or an energetic signal that we radiate or transmit to the environment and other people. It is a composite of the particular frequency or vibrations of our body, our mind, our heart, and our consciousness.

Research has also shown that all beings have the ability to control their vibration. Just as you might set your radio to a particular station by adjusting its frequency, you can attune to higher energetic vibrations by expanding your consciousness.

People who are truly conscious and aware have an energetic empowerment presence that creates an energy field of healing, nurturing, caring, creativity, expansiveness, and joyfulness. If you are going to create you as the source for creating a different world, you have to be willing to function at a bigger level than anybody else around you. This energy field has an energetic entrainment frequency and strongly affects others.

An elevated intensity of consciousness allows you to see different possibilities and thrive in these times of exponential change. Only through elevated conscious awareness can you fully explore, investigate, access, discover, and know what to do with the different possibilities that are available to you.

Unconscious or anti-conscious.

In the state of unconscious or anti-conscious, there is no connection, only separation. When leaders are unconscious or anti-conscious, they are living and functioning in a state of separation from the wholeness of life. When business leaders are operating anti-consciously, they tend to be motivated by selfishness and greed, which leads to exploitation, mishandling, abuse, and even fraud and deception.

A recent example of this is Volkswagen, where senior leaders allowed false readings on emissions testing and have admitted to rigging the software to pass emissions tests. The CEO and board claimed to be unaware of what had been going on for years—an example of unconscious leadership. The whole ordeal is going to cost the company over US$8 billion. This resulted from acting against the awareness of what society and the planet require and is an example of anti-conscious behavior.

According to *Fast Company*, "Although the German automaker has had a history of fostering a corporate culture that is 'cutthroat and insular,' Martin Winterkorn, who had been at the helm since 2007, may have contributed to the company's unethical and illegal installation of software that failed to accurately report emissions on its vehicles . . . Though he claimed not to be aware of the wrongdoing, Winterkorn is known as being a hard-driving perfectionist who would carry a gauge while he walked around to measure gaps between car doors in relentless pursuit of securing the top spot among global car manufacturers . . . His exacting standards, as well as his proclivity for calling employees out publicly to criticize them, may have very well motivated them to hide information in order to keep their jobs—or allowed them to believe it was okay to cheat, as long as it helped the company meet its lofty goals."

The culture created by an anti-conscious leader is typically autocratic, oppressive, and fear-driven—with attempts to control everything. There is a general underlying fear of invalidation and reprisals, and a distinct lack of sharing of information. The culture is one of right or wrong, good or bad, and is typified by the "you are either with me or against me" point of view.

What differentiates the conscious leader from an unconscious or anti-conscious leader is that the conscious leader doesn't have the necessity of proving that they are superior or greater than anyone else. Unconscious and anti-conscious leaders often "do" superiority because they are always trying to prove that they are not inferior and that they have value. It takes a great deal of energy to function in the state of unconscious or anti-conscious. This misuse of energy is a toxic and harmful force in personal and work life.

The source of transformation.

When you choose consciousness, your consciousness invades everything and everyone, and that, in turn, creates more consciousness, just like the large grandfather clocks. The more you choose consciousness, the more you will permeate other people's reality and the less they will be willing to hold on to their limitations. Your being conscious actualizes different possibilities. You become a catalyst for change. By choosing to be conscious and aware, you change everything and everyone around you.

One of the best examples is Herb Kelleher, co-founder, CEO, president, and chairman of Southwest Airlines. Kelleher brought a sense of purpose to the organization and motivated his employees to achieve a shared target by his power of presence. The U.S. Department of Transportation affirmed that Southwest had become the dominant carrier in the nation's busiest air travel markets and was the "principal driving force for changes occurring in the airline industry."

Kelleher's leadership flair is seen as the driving force of this unconventional airline, which has consistently posted a profit for 26 consecutive years and does things differently than any other company in the industry. In 1998, Southwest Airlines was named the best place to work in America by *Fortune* magazine; twenty years later, in 2018, it was voted the best U.S. carrier by TripAdvisor. To an extreme degree, Kelleher has made working in the business an adventure for his people. The culture of the organization is characterized by a focus on integrity, trust, creativity, intuition, innovation, freedom, flexibility, and generosity.

Kelleher is influential and inspirational. He provides visions that transform the way people think about what is possible, feasible, and attainable. The key to Southwest's success is largely thought to be the warmth and determination of its employees, who mirror those same qualities in their leader. Wall Street wizards who have followed Southwest for years credit the airline's success to Kelleher's unorthodox personality and engaging leadership style.

Kelleher believes in infinite possibilities. He seeks and maximizes opportunity and is able to perceive and work with risk. A Harvard Business School case study of Southwest said the airline had succeeded in "differentiating itself through its focus on service, operations, cost control, marketing, its people, and its corporate culture, where kindness and the human spirit are nurtured." Unlike workers at most other carriers, Southwest employees are willing to go the extra mile and pitch in wherever needed.

The old-fashioned loyalty between employees and employer may have disappeared elsewhere in corporate America, but it is stronger than ever at Southwest. According to Steve Lewins, a Gruntal & Co. analyst who has been monitoring Kelleher's moves almost since Southwest began flying in 1971, "I think Herb is brilliant, charming, cunning, and tough. He is the sort of leader who will stay out with a mechanic in some bar until four o'clock in the morning to find out what is going on. And then he will fix whatever is wrong."

The capacity of Southwest to thrive and out-create other businesses depends on Kelleher's ability to transcend his preconceived notions, rise above everyone else's best practices, go beyond all the expert opinions, and triumph over his own doubt. Because of vision, inventiveness, resourcefulness, nonconformity, unconventionality, creative talent, and generative ability, conscious leaders become the source of substantial transformation for their organization.

Kelleher revealed that higher levels of conscious choice and intensity of awareness are the keys to creating a balanced integration of organizational vision and strategic and operational realities. If you are willing to be a conscious leader in the world, everything is possible. If you choose to be a conscious leader, you must believe and know that you are, and you must perceive and receive that you are. Soon, the conditions of your reality will change to entrain with your consciousness. The true source of consciousness is choice. Only you can validate your consciousness, and you do that by the choice you make.

Be the gift of change.

When you are totally conscious, you have a perception of full awareness, of being in communion with all of life. Oppositely, when you are totally contracted and unaware, you become unconscious, energy dense, and resistant of everyone and everything. This wisdom reminds me of the parable of the rainmaker, told by Carl Jung:

> A certain province in China, where the missionary Richard Wilhelm lived, was suffering a terrible drought. They had tried all the usual magical charms and rites to produce rain, but to no avail. There had not been a drop of rain, and the situation became catastrophic. Then someone said there was a rainmaker in a distant province, who was known to be effective in producing rain. The local dignitaries invited him and sent a carriage to bring him to the drought-stricken area.
>
> In time the rainmaker arrived and was greeted by the local

dignitaries, who pleaded with him to help produce rain. The rainmaker closed his eyes, breathed in the air, then opened his eyes, looked around, and pointed to a small cottage high up on the side of a mountain. He asked if he could reside there for a few days. The officials agreed and the rainmaker went up and locked himself in the cottage. Three days later, storm clouds gathered and there was a torrential downpour. The inhabitants were jubilant, and a delegation, led by the officials, went up to the cottage to thank the rainmaker. The rainmaker shook his head and said, "But I didn't make it rain."

The officials said he must have done it, as three days had passed since he arrived in the village and rain had been produced. The rainmaker replied, "Oh, I can explain that. I come from a country where things are in harmony with the universe. We have sunshine, we have rain. Here things are out of harmony, they are not in accord with the order of the universe, and I, too, was disturbed. I went to the cottage to set myself straight and once I was back in harmony, the rain came naturally."

The rainmaker was willing to create himself as the source for creating a different reality. He was willing to function at a more generative energy than anybody else in the village. He was willing to be the catalyst for change and for different possibilities in the world.

If you are going to create you as the catalyst for change and for different possibilities, you have to be willing to be conscious and to function at a more generative level than anybody else around you. What would it be like if you were actually willing to be the gift of change you truly are?

Like the rainmaker, when you expand your intensity of consciousness, you expand your energetic empowerment and create a stirring of energetic entrainment throughout your organization. You become the source of an organization's success, achievements, joy, brilliance, and prosperity. When you choose consciousness, those around you share the rewards. Consciousness is the antidote to autopilot or unconscious mode.

From this space of being, you are able to access real-world knowledge of your industry, global trends, and possible futures. You are able to perceive and receive all the new opportunities that hyper-innovation, rapid social change, and technological progress generate.

A creator of a different possibility.

Conscious leaders live their life and lead their business from infinite choice and infinite possibilities. They wish everyone well. They operate from an awareness of how their actions contribute to them personally *and* to everybody else. This ability is imperative for personal and professional success. It doesn't matter whether you're the president of a country, a chief executive officer, a board director, a supervisor, a manager, or a house husband.

We have observed the power of conscious leaders at work over and over again in all kinds of businesses, large and small. When we see the results of amazingly successful organizations, we know we are witnessing the work of conscious leaders. We have seen that the chief executives, boards, and leadership teams who have embraced a conscious awareness way of being and leading have a profound effect on the ability of organizations to perform effectively.

When we choose to live and lead with conscious awareness, we can become architects or catalysts for making the world a better place. We can contribute to the greater good. Clara Barton was an example of this. She showed that if you are truly the creator source of your life, you get to choose anything and everything.

Barton was an unusual woman for her time (1821–1912). In those days, most women were expected to marry, have children, and stay home to take care of them. Barton, however, did not allow herself to operate within the limitations of this reality or be bound by what is. She operated from the question, what possibility do I have here?

Barton began life as a shy child but went on boldly to serve her community and country in ways few people before her had ever tried. She went to a special school for girls in Massachusetts. While in that school, she became interested in public education. She knew what she would like to create as her life and what she had to do to get there. She wanted to share the gift of education, so she founded a public school in New Jersey.

During that period, people thought education was only for children whose parents had enough money to pay for private schools. Bureaucrats did not want Barton to start a school for poor people, but she refused to let bureaucracy stifle her awareness. She was choosing for her regardless of what anybody else said. She had to transcend other people's preconceived notions, rise above everyone else's judgment, and triumph over their doubt.

Clara offered to teach without pay for three months and the officials could choose after that if she could continue. They gave her an old building with poor equipment. And they gave her six very active little boys to teach. By the end of three months the school became too small for the number of children who wanted to attend. By the end of the year, the town built her a bigger, better school, because she then had six hundred students in the school.

She became a teacher at an early age, and after sixteen years of teaching she realized she did not know all she wanted to know. She wanted more education. Very few universities accepted women in those days. Barton, however, knew what was true for her and she chose to be that, whether anybody else went for it or not. In this type of situation, attitude and high level of conscious awareness mean everything.

Barton later became one of the first women employees in the federal government. According to National Women's History museum, "In 1854 she was hired as a recording clerk at the U.S. Patent Office in Washington, DC, the first woman appointed to such a post. She was paid $1,400 annually, the same as her male colleagues. However, the following year, Secretary of the Interior Robert McClelland, who opposed women working in government, reduced her to copyist with a lower salary. In 1857, the Buchanan Administration eliminated her position entirely, but in 1860, she returned as copyist after the election of President Abraham Lincoln."

When the Civil War began in 1861, Barton made it her mission to bring medical supplies to Union soldiers in need. She became a head nurse in 1864—even though she had no formal medical training. She soon found herself working to aid the soldiers on the front lines. In one instance, she was able to support surgeons on the front line with replenishments when they had run out of supplies. Barton's efforts earned her the nickname "Angel of the Battlefield."

After the Civil War, Barton supervised a federal search to locate missing soldiers and delivered speeches on war experiences. Later, building off her nursing experience, she was a pioneer and innovator in transforming health care. She was always willing to create things beyond what anybody else could comprehend—willing to out-create other people's need to hold things in place.

The 1864 Geneva Convention had established the International Red Cross, and though the U.S. had not participated in the Convention, Barton began to lobby for the establishment of an American branch of the Red Cross, winning support from Cabinet and Congress members. In 1881, the National Society of the Red Cross was established one block from the White House, and Barton served as the agency's active president for 23 years, retiring in 1904 at age 82. Clara never gave up, she never gave in, she never quit. She showed us that when we have our own reality, we don't have to buy anybody else's point of view—ever. If we keep on going and we keep on trying, eventually we will be successful.

Barton had the awareness to know what was happening and function in the moment, where she could change anything as needed to accomplish and create more. No one and nothing was more valuable than her consciousness and her choice. Most important, she never gave up her point of view for somebody else's.

Her willingness to be aware of everything allowed her to perceive different possibilities. She never lived her life by somebody else's reality, so she always had total choice. Barton became deeply involved in the world because she was willing to be aware of other possibilities. She had the awareness to know what was happening and therefore was able to generate something different. If we see having this kind of intensity of awareness as a real possibility, imagine what we could create with our business.

Ultimately, consciousness is a way of connecting with what is happening at the present moment and with the infinite possibilities that are always available. Consciousness is an ever-expanding level of possibility that includes everything—without judgment. When you are willing to be totally conscious, you can receive everything. And because you can receive everything, your awareness expands.

Be the willingness to expand your awareness. This allows you to have total choice. From this expanded awareness space, you have infinite choice and infinite possibilities. Consciousness is a way of connecting what is happening at the present moment with the infinite possibilities.

EIGHT

Being the Energy and Following the Energy

This is the willingness to be an energy that cannot be confined, defined, or limited. It's being all the awareness you are. It's being the question that creates the catalyst, the contribution, and the possibilities in other people's worlds by the fact that you are not definable or confinable. Being the energy and the vibration of a conscious leader, having the willingness to not cut off your gift or anything you are capable of, means you can choose to be, do, have, create, and generate everything that is possible.

Being the energy of a conscious leader is not about what you have to *do*, and you certainly don't have to figure out *how*. It is simply allowing yourself to *be the energy, space, and consciousness* that a conscious leader is. No conclusion, no fixed point of view, no restrictions, no limitations—just choice, question, and possibility. When we make a choice to step into being the energy and the vibration of a conscious leader, we simply become that energy. You become a creator of a different possibility when you are being the conscious leader. So ask yourself, "What generative energy, space, and consciousness can I and my body be that would allow me to be the conscious leader that I truly *can* be?"

Quantum physics has discovered that the essential nature of the universe is the movement of energy and information. There is nothing other than energy and information; all things exist through their communion and interaction. Leading with conscious awareness is about following energy rather than using force and effort as a way of making things occur in your life. If you are willing to follow the energy, then you don't have to constantly micromanage your life. When you follow the energy, you don't have to control everything; you can simply allow the energy to lead you into a different possibility in life.

Energy is something you can be aware of. It's something you can be, it's something you can connect with, it's something you can direct, influence, change, and employ. When you start looking at yourself, at your life, your business, and your future as an energy, you begin to have a greater awareness of possibilities—ways to be, choices you have, directions you can take, and different possibilities you can generate.

Following the energy.

Conscious leaders create their lives consciously by following the energy—by consciously being and asking questions and then making conscious choices moment-to-moment based on the information and awareness they perceive. Following the energy is about being willing to receive the information that is available. It is about being open to infinite choice and infinite possibilities. It involves asking questions so that your awareness and the universe has an avenue for responding. The world is an unlimited place with unlimited possibilities that provide unlimited opportunities if we be the question. When you are the question and you choose something, you create multiple possibilities.

To some extent, the same is true whether you are leading a country or community, creating or leading a business, or investing in the stock market or properties. If you follow the energy and function from *what else is possible*, you are in a state of expansiveness of what can truly be. When you follow the energy, you're choosing to have true choice. It's not about making a right or a wrong choice—it's simply, "Okay, what is possible here?"

If you would like the future to be full of ever-expanding possibilities and unlimited choices, you have to be willing to be the energy that creates everything you would like to have—instead of trying to do what's right or predictable or controllable. All the magical things that happen in life occur when you follow the energy and function from *what else is possible*. There is no energy that is unavailable to you if you choose to perceive, know, be, and receive it. Energy is the substance by which transformation occurs. Energy is present, mutable, and changeable upon request. If you are willing to be aware of energy and follow the energy of life, you will perceive and receive something greater than you have previously been willing to receive.

Your ability to follow the energy is everything when it comes to leading a successful business. Look at the lives of the most successful people in their fields. You will very often find that they follow the energy and choose based on what's going to be most expansive for them and for everyone concerned. The takeaway is that when you are willing to follow the energy, you *can* receive everything. And because you can receive everything, your awareness expands.

The world is full of choices and possibilities.

When you follow the energy, you are aware whether your choice will be expansive and create more possibilities or whether it will be contractive and create limitation for you and everyone else. This awareness greatly enhances the potentiality and probability of your success. A great example of this in the business arena is Richard Branson. Branson is known for his adventurous spirit and sporting achievements, including crossing oceans in a hot air balloon.

Branson has chosen to totally function from infinite choice and infinite possibilities without conclusion or fixed points of view. He's willing to receive everything and anything, to see different possibilities with no judgment of good or bad. He does not fit the mold of a businessperson, yet he is a very successful business entrepreneur. When Branson started Virgin from a basement in West London, there was no great plan or strategy. He just followed the energy. He didn't set out to build a business empire, and he has never gone into any of his businesses just to make money. For him, building a business is all about doing something to be proud of, bringing talented people together, and creating something that's going to make a real difference to other people's lives. His success comes from setting huge, apparently unachievable challenges and trying to rise above them. His attitude has always been without fear of failure. If he falls flat on his face, at least he's moving forward. All he has to do is get back up and try again.

According to Branson, every Virgin product and service has been made to make a positive difference in people's lives. By following the energy and focusing on being the catalyst for different possibilities, Virgin has been able to build a wildly successful group of companies. Branson said, "I've seen life as one long learning process. And if I see, you know, if I fly on somebody else's airline and find the experience is not a pleasant one . . . then I'd think, well, you know, maybe I can create the kind of airline that I'd like to fly on."

He doesn't live his life by other people's points of view, nor does he do what everybody else says is the right and correct way. He always follows the energy and spontaneously fosters a different way of seeing and being in the world. He sees the world with a different eye. He sees infinite choice and infinite possibility without coming to conclusion. There is no sense of lack in his world; instead, there is a sense of ease. His point of view is like, "Oh well, I'll get that, one way or another." That's what life is like for Branson. He has total choice because he knows the world is full of choices, possibilities, and opportunities.

Branson continues to generate different possibilities because he is the energy of a catalyst for a different possibility. To him, a business has to be involving, it has to be fun, and it has to exercise creative instincts. He has said, "I'm not the sort of person who gives up on things. The first time we crossed the Atlantic in the balloon, it crashed, and we went on and did the Pacific. First time we crossed the Atlantic in a boat, it sank, and we went on and got the record. So, generally speaking, we will pick ourselves up, brush ourselves down, and carry on."

Opening doors to the world of infinite possibilities

Your awareness of energy gives you information about what is and opens doors to the world of infinite possibilities. From that space of being, you have choice. Engaging your innate ability to perceive, know, be, and receive the energy of the universe is your ticket to total awareness. It allows you to operate in a highly creative space beyond the controls and restraints of your cognitive or rational mind.

From my own personal experience, making a conscious choice to add this ability to my business skillset was a choice that changed my business and financial life substantially and remarkably. My awareness of energy gives me information about what is truly going on in the world and opens doors to the world of infinite possibilities. From that space of being, I truly have choice. Ability to follow the energy allows me to operate in a highly creative and generative space beyond the controls and restraints of my cognitive or rational mind.

The interesting part about being the chief financial officer of our seven global businesses is the need to straddle the financial stewardship and the strategic and business leadership—with direct responsibility in shaping the business strategies in light of highly uncertain macroeconomic environments. When I start looking at my life as an energy, at the things I desire to bring into my life and my business as an energy, it starts giving me this whole other awareness of possibilities of ways to be and of things I can generate.

As chief financial officer, I am responsible for our personal and business financial reality, and I am in charge of making choices on how to invest the money, taking into consideration risk, possibilities, and liquidity. In the current environment, I often have to make decisions quickly and strategically, oftentimes without the research and context that other people insist are prerequisites for business decisions. By following the energy and using my awareness extensively to manage our investments, I am able to stop investing with my emotions and my head and create investments that most people could never imagine.

Following the energy is about being and asking questions so that my awareness has an avenue for responding. Being the energy and following the energy allows me to be totally present, to function in the simultaneity of past, present, and future and thus not be influenced unconsciously by past events or future concerns. Before I educated myself to follow the energy, I was quick to get excited when the markets were rising and often jumped in at the top of a bull market. Then, as the inevitable regression followed, fear of loss prompted me to sell at a market low. Most people who have bought or sold stocks have done similar things.

For years I have been studying leadership, business, and behavioral finance. I have observed and analysed many theories and models that use objective data to predict how markets will respond under certain circumstances. The reality is, these models are erroneous and unreliable, because there are too many anomalies that conventional models cannot explain. It's clearly impossible to predict every crazy, unconscious, and senseless move investors might make; it's also impossible to know everything about a stock before buying or selling. But functioning from question, choice, possibility, and contribution will help ensure you're investing based on awareness and objective knowledge rather than your own assumptions, conclusions, or emotions.

Question, choice, possibility, and contribution are the four elements of how I grow our investments and lead our businesses. I ask myself daily, "What's really possible here? What would I like to create here? What choices do I have? What contribution can I be or receive to bring that into existence?" These questions put me on the conscious leadership edge of a different reality. This is an ever-expanding universe that I can choose to step into at will. When I ask a nonlinear and unlimited question and I don't have a preconceived idea of an expected outcome or answer, I create the space for receiving insights otherwise unattainable.

Stop being obsessed with getting the right answer

Being the question does not mean trying to get to the right answer or the right solution. It means using questions to bypass the limited answers your mind provides. When I make a choice to invest in something, I always ask, "What is possible beyond this reality that I have available to me that I have not yet chosen?" Or, "What else is possible that I haven't considered?" Questions destabilize fixed points of view and shake the mind loose from its presumptions. They impel your mind beyond the rut of timeworn blueprints. Unlimited questions are far more valuable than the so-called "right" answers, because they open the door to all possibility.

When it comes to finances and investment success, you will often find that the difference between success and failure is determined by whether someone is functioning from conclusion. You eliminate possibilities every time you come to any conclusion. For example, you might decide, "I don't want to invest in this business because I don't like the CEO." Is that a conclusion? Yes. Does that avoid any possibilities? Yes, indeed. Why? Because that one conclusion, that one decision, that one judgment, eliminates anything that doesn't match your conclusion. Anytime you make a judgment, a decision, or a conclusion, nothing that does not match it can come into your awareness or your life.

This is a radical idea for most people to receive. But in my view, it is vital. One of the major challenges facing leaders today is learning to let go of control—to stop trying to get to the right answer or the right solution. Have you ever heard conventional leaders emphasize that good leaders must have the right answer, the right choice, and take decisive action? I have. In fact, I was told by my boss many years ago that having the right answer was necessary in order to progress! Most of us have been trained to believe that correct judgment will lead to the correct choice; if we choose the right thing, then everything will turn out exactly the way we want. If you subscribe to this point of view, you will always try to choose based on the correct choice, the right choice, the good choice.

But what if there is no wrong choice?

When you are obsessed with getting the "right" answer and the "right" choice, to avoid making the "wrong" choice you will constantly be doubting and judging every choice you make. Whenever you expect to have the right answer or the right choice, you limit what it can be and what you can receive. The habit of excessively needing to be right and get the right answer impedes your ability to see what is actually in front of you. What if there is no wrong choice? When you lead your life and your business by following the energy, it's not about making a right or a wrong choice. It's simply, "Okay, what do I want to choose here?"

When you choose to follow the energy and live your life from that energy, there is no investment in the outcome and no idea of what might show up; there is only awareness of the energy. It is based on continuous questioning and following the energy and readying yourself for whatever may show up. Then, be willing and ready to go wherever things are going. Be ready to act.

Following the energy allows you to be in a constant state of possibility and choosing a possibility that you have not yet considered. You will be able to achieve more generative outcomes when you make decisions by following the energy and trusting your own awareness. This way of working is quite different from "thinking up an answer." You must trust that, by following the energy, the pieces will ultimately fit.

I have established that in order to expand my awareness I must release my judgment, projection, and expectation about the choices and the expected result, about how it is supposed to show up or what it must look like when it shows up. When I stop functioning from a fixed idea or concept of how things are supposed to be, I'm able to get to the place where I'm willing to have total choice and total possibility—with no point of view about how it shows up or what it looks like when it shows up.

I can't imagine where or who I'd be without the essential tool of *being the question*. Being the question and following the energy opens me up to infinite possibilities. It gives me access to infinite choices that I haven't considered. What I love most about being the question is it gives me the ability to have an ever-expanding awareness and consciousness, allowing me to create a thriving and joyful life instead of a predictable one.

Being the question has created amazing success for our businesses. For example, as part of our Conscious Governance Board consulting business, Steve and I knew there was something more possible in the field of strategic planning, an exercise that every organization goes through (albeit mostly very badly). Being the question made our strategic planning process quick and easy and very strategic, a most unusual set of characteristics. We introduced the paradigm of "Strategic Awareness"—where strategy and personal awareness work together to create something greater—into the business vocabulary. It has since become a major influence and contribution to the way businesses conduct strategic planning.

Strategic Awareness is now used globally to lead businesses out of traditional strategic planning processes and into innovative modes. This paradigm is a framework for moving people from the conclusion of what they've decided they want the future to be into new and different possibilities. And it all came about by us being the question at all times.

With Strategic Awareness as a key framework, a good deal of the work we do with CEOs, boards of directors, and senior leadership teams is focused on unlocking their awareness, inviting them to live in the question, strengthening their ability to perceive different possibilities, and cultivating more generative strategies from this space. This facilitates leadership teams to function from the awareness of what will create the future they would like to have for their enterprise, mapping out both strategic and tactical possibilities for getting there. Many of our clients have been able to generate growth and new possibilities greater than they've ever imagined.

NINE

Getting Started Is What Counts

Conscious leadership is not about superiority or competition. Being conscious does not make you superior; it just makes you more aware. When you are totally aware, you will not be an effect of anyone else's unconsciousness or anti-consciousness.

Conscious leadership is only a matter of choice. If you choose to be conscious, then you can be. The most important thing here is to get a very clear sense of where you are starting from. It is imperative to remove your limiting beliefs about leadership if you truly would like to be a conscious leader.

If you're like most business leaders, you have many points of view about leadership and business principles that you're not even aware you have. Before you set off expanding your conscious leadership abilities, you need to take a moment to become aware of your points of view about leadership. You also need to become aware of how these points of view may limit your performance. You will be a victim to your points of view if you are not aware of them.

Here's how to get started. Ask yourself these questions:

- What does leadership mean to me?

- What does it mean to be a conscious leader?

- What kind of leader am I now?

- Am I already a conscious leader?

- Do I have a sincere aspiration to become a conscious leader?

Reflect on your responses to the above questions. Are you willing to see that it's *not* what's in the world that limits the scope of your leadership ability—it's *your* unexamined points of view? Your point of view creates your reality.

Use your mind and your intellect to your advantage.

In this reality, the finite place people function from is thoughts, feelings, and emotions. It is essential to recognize that thoughts, feelings, and emotions are by-products of the mind, which is a regulating system of our life. The mind is a calculating system that defines what we are already familiar with; it defines the limitations of our reality. The mind gets in the way of knowing because it justifies everything leaders do and does nothing to create infinite possibilities.

Whether you realize it or not, you can choose to have your mind working for you, or it will inevitably control you and work against you. This happens when you function unconsciously (on autopilot mode). When you choose to function consciously, you are able to use your mind and your intellect to your advantage. When you choose to function unconsciously, your mind controls you by conditioning you to believe that you need to create your reality and your life from conclusion, projection, expectation, and judgment—that you could *not* simply do it from choice. The autopilot mode becomes your operative state of living. But your operative state is a place you can *choose*. It's a choice you make . . . autopilot or conscious?

As a leader, you can choose to have conscious, unconscious, or anti-conscious operative states of being. When you choose to be conscious, you have total awareness of what you could be, do, have, create, and generate. No boundaries, no limitations—just choice, question, and possibility. This is the place where you can create and generate what works for you.

When I talk about choosing to be unconscious, I'm talking about all the places where you make yourself unaware enough to accept the notion that being normal and average is the best and only way to be. When you choose an unconscious operative state of being, you give up your awareness in order to buy the rightness of this reality. You have to make yourself unaware and unconscious in order to choose the unconscious mode over total awareness. This is how you end up eliminating possibilities and never getting what you truly desire.

When you choose an anti-conscious operative state of being, you actively work against the consciousness of you and those around you. You create unhealthy climates in your home and your organization. When you choose an anti-conscious operative state of being, you tend to do everything anti-consciously with excessive control, effort, fixed points of view, conclusion, and forcefulness. Both unconscious and anti-conscious operative states are ways you create autopilot operative states of being. You never question these. This is just the way things are. When you are in these operative states, you are not operating on an expanded awareness level. This creates tremendous limitation.

The autopilot operative state of being is an unconscious conditioning held in place by your personal viewpoints, decisions, conclusions, projections, and judgments you have made and any points of view that are fixed. Unconscious conditioning hypnotizes you into an unconscious state and sets you up to automatically go into discernment or judgment, even discrimination. Whenever you make a judgment about anything, those things that do not match your judgment cannot come into your reality. Unconscious conditioning keeps you finite, limited, and contracted, extinguishing your ability to function from infinite choice and infinite possibilities.

Acknowledge what your existing beliefs are!

Many of the popular leadership styles and approaches have been developed around images of the spirited and audacious leader who is authoritative, decisive, and out in front leading the organization to victory. We have been conditioned by many influential images to think of the leader as always charismatic—the epitome of the one who knows best. Our internal beliefs concerning leadership and success have been ingrained into our perspective without us ever having realized it.

We all hold many fixed points of view. We reiterate to ourselves numerous internal dialogues about all kind of topics. For example, some people tell themselves lies about why they cannot be a leader, why they cannot succeed at business, why they are not a good communicator, or why they are not good with money and finance. These points of view and internal dialogues are like personal scripts that we tend to make factual. We use them to create our reality.

Every fixed point of view keeps you from seeing the path to possibility. The interesting thing is that these viewpoints are not necessarily true or untrue; rather, they merely represent views that we have crafted for ourselves, often based on our unconscious beliefs. In an effort to become leaders, we frequently hold untrue assumptions, projections, and expectations of how leaders should look, act, be, and behave. In effect, we sketch what we want to apply to ourselves, forming an image that meets that sketch. So, rather than become conscious and amazing, we join the popular ranks of the ordinary leaders who are unlikely to become conscious and amazing.

Whenever I talk about leadership and awareness, I'm reminded of a quote from Nelson Mandela: "It is what we make out of what we have, not what we are given, that separates one person from another. Peace is the greatest weapon for development that any people can have."

In working with leaders around the world, I have personally discovered that being a conscious leader is a choice. It is choosing to live in the world as the greatness you are, which invites everyone else to be the greatness they are. Being a conscious leader is about right here, right now. It occurs in the moment you choose to be all that is possible. When you are functioning consciously, you can become an architect for making the world a better place. You can contribute to the greater good. It's important to emphasize that becoming a conscious leader cannot and certainly will not happen without sincere desire and earnest choice.

Being a contribution to the greater good seems to come naturally to John Kelly, AM, the National CEO of the Heart Foundation of Australia. Steve and I have had the pleasure of knowing and working with John for decades and have seen him transform organizations in a way that is nothing short of miraculous. John's previous roles have included CEO of Aged & Community Services Australia, Chair of Royal College of Nursing Australia, and Commonwealth Aged Care Commissioner.

John chooses to be a conscious leader. He is one of these rare individuals who is aware of everything and judges nothing. He does not operate within the limitations that others create for him and themselves in business. He is masterful at demolishing organizational silos and has an amazing capacity for persuading entrenched executives to change their points of view.

The ability to trust in his awareness and insight has made John a super successful CEO and equally successful businessman. Instinctively, John knows what's possible—what he needs to be and do differently to release the organization he leads from its legacy of business-as-usual mindset. He has the ability to deal with very challenging situations in a way that few of us are able to match. As he functions from possibility and no judgment, he goes where others fear to go. This provides him the space to make those decisions that will create the required change, whether people go with him or not. As he has no judgment of this, he brings along people in a way that is magical.

Observing, questioning, and probing into the limitations of others is John's most remarkable capacity. He is not attached to outmoded business conventions or past reference points and seems always willing to take risks and abolish old systems, structures, and routines in order to create something greater. It's a kind of fearlessness and optimism and confidence that allows him to overcome a variety of obstacles in a variety of ways. His accomplishments demonstrate the efficacy of conscious leadership.

Most recently, John created and shaped the merger of six disparate state-based organizations under the one umbrella of National Heart Foundation. He took on hard decisions that were required to create the change necessary for the future of heart health in Australia. He did this in a way that was effective and relatively quick.

John never judges himself or others. Instead, he is aware of all the judgments surrounding him, and from that awareness he is able to create possibilities in a way that few have been able to achieve.

Everything that you are, you have created!

You are the creator of everything that is expansive and everything that is contracted about your life. In one way or another, you create everything that you have in your life that doesn't work or is not so good. These could be relationship problems, work predicaments, physical pain, or financial dilemmas. You create these through your fixed points of view, thoughts, feelings, and emotions—and through your spoken words.

As you think and as you speak, you create a vibration. Every thought and every word has a vibration, an electrical, energetic component that creates your reality. These are exactly the parameters from which you create your life. Every time you think, "I am . . . " that is exactly what you become. For example, if you think that you are worthless, you are going to create a low self-regard and miserable life. If you think anti-conscious thoughts, you are going to feel dismal, pathetic, and contracted. If your thoughts are based on scarcity and lack, you will always have no abundance. Is it any wonder that the bulk of people subsist in a scarcity paradigm? Not realizing it, they choose to believe in "lack of" and "there is not enough to go around." They fail to recognize that they possess the unlimited power to choose.

It is crucial to acknowledge that the occurrences and the state of affairs in your life are thoughts first before they develop into reality.

For example, your financial condition is a thought first that then manifests into a reality. If you want to have a more expansive existence and abundant financial picture, you must first look at your thoughts and consciously choose more expansive thoughts.

You have to take responsibility for what you are thinking and what you are saying. The responsibility is acknowledging that *you* are creating this and *you* have the power to choose. The greatest power that you possess is the power to choose with awareness. When you function with awareness, you don't have any fixed thoughts, just awareness. Awareness allows you to function with no limitation and fixed point of view, so choices can be made instantaneously.

When you chose to be a conscious leader, you don't have the point of view that anything will ever stop you. You are the question that would allow you to see different possibilities that weren't visible previously. A magnificent example of this is Nelson Mandela. He has inspired me, like millions around the world, to see the possibilities and the questions in everything, to forgive, not to foster hate and bitterness, not to be controlled by projections, expectations, and judgments, and to never come to conclusion. Mandela chose to be everything he was, regardless of whether anybody else went along with it.

Mandela encapsulates this way of being. He said, "Everyone can rise above their circumstances and achieve success if they are dedicated to and passionate about what they do and have a fundamental concern for others. There is no passion to be found playing small—in settling for a life that is less than the one you are capable of living."

Where are you operating from?

You must get clear about where you are operating from. Are you leading your life and your business with awareness? Are you looking at creating something greater? Over and over again, I have observed that when leaders do not take the important step of examining themselves, they can be blinded by their limitations. We need to get clear about where we are operating from. We have to be willing to be aware of what's going on. By examining and acknowledging our current operative state of being—by acknowledging *what is*—we can begin to recognize that we can create a different reality.

When we are in an autopilot operative state, we are not operating on an aware level. We are operating on autopilot. Are you functioning from a state you think you have to operate from rather than having a choice or possibility? Are you trying to create from autopilot mode as though that's the only choice there is?

The fundamental process is to recognize and acknowledge what your existing operative states of being are. When you acknowledge your existing limited beliefs and fixed points of view, it no longer has a fixed form. Is now the time to become a catalyst for change and for different possibilities? What if the only thing stopping you from changing everything right now is the belief that you can't? Every belief is a limitation.

If you have a belief that "being a catalyst for change and for different possibilities has to happen like this" or "things have to look a certain way before I can be a conscious leader," you miss possibilities. You don't notice the possibilities showing up in your life right now that could allow you to be a catalyst for change and for different possibilities.

If you don't believe you can ever be a conscious leader, the chances are you never will be. Your beliefs control everything you do and everything you create. Your reality is the way you perceive and feel about yourself at any point in time, and your points of view are the things that lock you into your reality. They are the basis upon which your life is created. Your own viewpoints and attitudes are the most powerful influencers in your life. So, it is vital to remove your limiting beliefs about you, the definition of you, and any definition you have about what it means to be a conscious leader.

Becoming a conscious leader is more than a matter of learning a variety of tools and practices. It is also a matter of believing that *it is truly possible*. Why is that? Because your beliefs and points of view determine your choices, and your choices determine your actions. If you desire to become a catalyst for a different possibility in the world, you have to be willing to believe that it is truly possible.

A shining example of this is Malala Yousafzai, the young Pakistani woman who became a spokesperson for women's education. Her advocacy has grown into an international movement. In retaliation for her high-profile campaign for women's education, she was shot in the head at close range by a Taliban gunman. She survived the gunshot wound and has become a leading spokesperson for education, women's rights, and human rights. She has received numerous peace awards and received the Nobel Peace Prize in 2014. Her belief that change was truly possible, and her point of view that judges no one, not even her attacker, has created a beacon of possibility in our world.

Yousafzai illustrates that if you are willing to see that the choices you make *can* create huge change, different realities will show up for you because you're *willing* to change. Unconsciousness cannot survive in the face of consciousness. When you choose consciousness, your consciousness invades everything and everyone—in turn creating more consciousness.

Don't let your limiting beliefs and doubts prevent you from becoming a conscious leader. Doubt is what we use to eliminate awareness and everything we know. Why would you choose that? What would it be like to create greater awareness instead of greater doubt? If you don't believe that you have abilities and competencies to become a conscious leader and the catalyst for a different possibility in the world, you certainly won't be creating any new possibilities. Your point of view determines your reality.

You contract yourself in order to maintain limiting beliefs and doubts. You only see what your doubt has decided should be or has to be. As long as you are hanging on to your doubt, you cannot truly see what is. But as you start to eliminate your doubt, you begin to see what is.

If you are feeling stuck in your life and want to change, start by becoming aware of your beliefs and doubts. I have discovered that new and different possibilities are often hiding behind our beliefs and doubts. How many operative states of limitation, unconsciousness, and anti-consciousness are you choosing? What can you change here? What else is possible? What choices do you have that could change this? What creation would you have available to you here if you were willing to embrace the energy, space, and consciousness of a conscious leader?

Be the questions and never come to any conclusion. You simply have to be willing to be aware of what's going on and have the awareness of where you are operating from. Examine what is in your life that you have been unwilling or unable to change that you would actually like to change. Would you be willing to *actually* have that change?

Be aware of your assumptions, conclusions,
projections, and expectations

We all have a tendency toward conclusion, assumption, projection, expectation, judgment, and rejection. It's just how our minds work when
we function on autopilot. But if you have no projections, expectations,
separations, judgments, or rejections, your awareness will expand exponentially. If you have no points of view, you can be aware of everything. On the flip side, as long as you're judging anyone or anything,
you can never see what's actually true.

Most of us don't realize how much our conclusions, projections,
and expectations determine our conduct and action. Many of us don't
realize how destructive and limiting our conclusions, projections, and
expectations can be. To truly become a conscious leader, you must
change the way you think about leadership. You may not even inten-
tionally or consciously have many points of view about leadership, but
unconsciously you surely have an operative state of being that is creating your reality right now. Be willing to change all this to unleash the
gift you can be to the world as a conscious leader.

What if you didn't look through your conclusions, projections,
expectations, separations, judgments, or rejections? Projections and expectations are never reality! They are just projections and expectations,
nothing more. When you get rid of your need to project, it puts you in
a constant state of creating.

There's an old adage about what happens when you assume something: You make an ass out of you and me. What this implies about
the liability and danger of making assumptions is valid. Whenever you
make assumptions of any kind, you ignore anything that would give

you awareness. You eliminate your awareness of different choices and different possibilities.

These words—assumption, conclusion, projection, expectation—are not words to be taken lightly. Your assumptions, conclusions, projections, and expectations about your business determine how you create it, operate it, and relate to it. Many great organizations have been crippled by leaders who focus on specializing, refuse to be aware of the new hyper-changing world, and continue to manage their business as usual. The board and executive leadership team at Kodak embraced assumption, conclusion, projection, and expectation, trapping themselves in the fixed points of view of their past success. They made judgment calls, trade-offs, and compromises that harmed their organization.

Being and acknowledging our capacity to create.

Don't make assumptions more real than your capacity to create. Assumptions eliminate our awareness and our capacity to create. When business leaders operate based on assumptions, conclusions, projections, and expectations, they tend to demonstrate lack of awareness, short-sightedness of vision, and superficiality in their priorities. The point is not to be the victim of our assumptions, conclusions, projections, and expectations, since these tend to paralyze us.

To do anything well requires being and acknowledging our capacity. If we don't see what we are capable of, if we don't see the gifts we have, then we can't use the capacity for us. Our actual capacity is the talent and ability we have. Fully acknowledging, claiming, and owning our capacity to be, do, have, create, and generate *anything* is an essential aspect of being a conscious leader. It is how one takes the step from just leading and managing to truly being a conscious leader.

Conscious leaders have to be good at being aware. Leadership without awareness and without the willingness to be, do, have, create, and generate anything isn't leadership. Leaders don't necessarily have to always have ingenious or groundbreaking ideas, but they have to be willing to recognize that they have the capacity to be creative and generative. In fact, if they don't have a true sense of mastery of their capacity to be creative and generative, they will never do what they are capable of doing.

The liability and danger of making assumptions.

Our assumptions and points of view about our business determines how we create it, operate it, and relate to it. When we see success through the filter of the "right way to do things," we have already decided what the right result is supposed to be. We eliminate the awareness of the possibilities we actually have.

If we operate based on our assumptions and conclusions, we have a tendency to align the present and future business with the practices of the past. Being captivated by the success of the past can easily destroy our awareness and lock us, contentedly, in place. We will cling to familiar turf. We assume that we must concentrate our efforts and try to compete in the markets our business is currently succeeding in, rather than accessing our capacity to be creative and generative. We judge our future potential through the filter of our past success, and we cut off our awareness of everything else. This places organizations in jeopardy.

Huge problems arise when we create our business in the context of fixed structures—when we attempt to compete only within the structure of our industry. Instead of asking what the possibilities are, these leaders have already decided what it is going to be. This is the way most leaders of many derailed companies demolished their businesses.

Leaders who derailed tend to make assumptions when they don't fully understand a situation. They often assume that something will happen, but in the end the total opposite does. As long as leaders are practicing assumption, conclusion, projection, or expectation, they can never see what's actually true. In effect, what they do is put on the filters of their preconceptions. If leaders have no assumptions or conclusions or projections about anything, then they get to look at everything for what it is, not for what they want it to be, not for what it ought to be. Just for what it is.

For example, if leaders decide that the past results from their products or services are outstanding, they become unwilling to see when the products become passé and outmoded. The moment leaders judge their products, services, or business model to be right or perfect, they stop perceiving what else is possible. They can't see anything else; they can't perceive or receive any other information. The Kodak leadership team made this mistake. They saw the future as a version of their past success rather than accepting that the digital photography revolution could totally change and restructure their industries.

Kodak's leaders never fully grasped how the world around them was changing. They were not choosing to be fully aware of future trends and how these trends would affect their business. They were closing their eyes to forewarning indications and hoping that things didn't change too much. They were not willing to break with their own successful practices. They hung on to obsolete assumptions about who took pictures, why, and when. As a direct result of this unconscious assumption, a once mighty organization declared bankruptcy.

There are few corporate slipups as astounding as Kodak's missed opportunities in digital photography—a technology that they invented. In 1976, Kodak invented and built the first digital camera. They owned the IP; they had the first mover advantage. This company should have owned it all. Instead, in 2012, Kodak filed for bankruptcy, having lost their dominance over the very technology they had invented.

Conscious leaders must be willing to acknowledge change. Kodak's leaders knew all about the impending rise of digital technology and how it threatened the company's stronghold. A report circulated among senior executives in 1979 detailing how the market would shift permanently from film to digital by 2010. But since the leadership team saw the future as a continuation of the past and present, they did not choose to keep pace with the emerging digital technology. They were not open to change and couldn't envision how significantly the entire industry was changing.

Kodak's leaders were convinced that digital cameras wouldn't have traction outside of the professional market. With this assumption and conclusion, they failed to see that the world would go as thoroughly digital as it has. They decided they weren't going to be in the digital camera business. As a result, they stopped devoting resources to digital and eliminated new products, new markets, and new opportunities from their possible pipeline.

Kodak's leadership team might have been able to achieve a different outcome if they proactively exited their legacy businesses in a timely way. Just because Kodak was in the paper-and-chemicals business didn't mean they couldn't be something else. Yet they concluded and assumed that their structure around chemicals and paper was so inflexible that any major change was unfathomable. There was no system within Kodak to allow flexibility and nimbleness. With the conclusion, assumption, and projection that their structure was solid and fixed in stone and that it would cost too much to change, they set up the conditions of "no choice." They concluded they had no other choice but to continue the same way and hope for the best.

The leadership team judged that any major change would take a long time, similar to past experiences. They concluded that they were right, that they were too big to fail, and that the market was theirs. The leaders couldn't see the fundamental shift happening right under their noses. They were looking for a conclusion rather than asking a question that would create a possibility they had never considered. Do you see that when you make assumptions you have to function in conclusion and rejection? You have no other choice.

Kodak exemplified that bringing the dead weight of past legacy into the future can be detrimental to a business. Many organizations have derailed badly because they did not recognize they had made certain assumptions. In other words, it was their unconscious assumptions that cost them severely. Whenever you make unconscious assumptions of any kind, you are creating failure—not success.

It is important to recognize that when we make an assumption about something, we're accepting it as true without actually finding proof. Preoccupation with assumption can seduce us into believing that all the details are not worth our attention. If Kodak's leaders had looked at all their assumptions, conclusions, projections, and expectations about the market and any conclusions they had about choice or no-choice, turned those assumptions into change possibilities and instituted some of the changes as well as continuing what they had, the situation may well have been different. They did none of these and thus were stuck in the no-choice universe.

Most businesses see the disruptive forces affecting their industry. They frequently divert sufficient resources to participate in emerging markets. Failure results from an inability to truly embrace the new business models that disruptive change opens up. Kodak created a digital camera, invested in the technology, and even understood that photos would be shared online. Where they failed was in realizing that online photo sharing was the new business, not just a way to expand the printing business.

The moment you make assumptions, conclusions, projections, or expectations, you cut off your awareness. You have to always be in question. You have to ask, "What's really going on here?" *Be in question.* We advise businesses to ask the following questions:

- What if our industry was very different from what it is now?

- What would we need to change so that, even if nothing changed, we would be better placed for the future?

- What have we decided we have right that will stop us from seeing other possibilities?

- What is happening now and into the future that, if we were to take note, would change the way we created our business?

Unconscious or anti-conscious leaders tend to function based on assumption, conclusion, projection, or expectation in order to have predictability, stability, constancy, and safety in their lives. As you aim to expand your ability to be a conscious leader, attachment to assumption, conclusion, projection, and expectation is one of the most restricting forces that diminishes your power.

The most important thing you can do is become fully aware of the assumptions, conclusions, projections, and expectations that you have been functioning from. This will give you an idea about how you have been creating your life and your business. Without this awareness it's easy to fall prey to the manner in which assumptions dictate your habitual behaviors.

Here are some questions for you:

- How many reference points, assumptions, conclusions, projections, and expectations do you have to hold you back?

- To what extent are you and your business operating according to outmoded practices, policies, and systems based on your assumptions, conclusions, projections, and expectations?

- How many systems and structures used in your life and your organization exist because they have always been done that way?

All things become possible when you're willing to have the awareness of all things that are possible. My question to you is this: "What assumptions, conclusions, projections, and expectations are you making on a daily basis that need to be questioned?" The more you consciously question your assumptions the more likely you are to deal with facts instead of fiction. And that has to be good for business.

Conscious leadership is only a matter of choice.

Being a conscious leader is something you choose. It is a choice you make. If you choose to be conscious, then you can be. If you choose to be unconscious or anti-conscious, then you can be that as well.

With the power to choose, you can choose to have infinite choice and infinite possibilities—or scarcity and lack. You can choose to be conscious in the moment, where you can change anything as needed to accomplish and create more, or you can choose to operate from anti-conscious viewpoints, with a fixed view of how things are supposed to be. You can choose to embody and be in the generative energy, space, and consciousness of *what else is possible*, or you can choose to function from conclusion and spend your life trying to create an end result of some kind.

If you are choosing to be a conscious leader and to create *you* as the source for creating a different world, then you have to be willing to be the power and potency that changes reality. The one thing you can always change is you. All you can do is be and do something different to change you. And changing you will change everyone and everything around you.

The remainder of this book will explore the three key elements of conscious leadership:

Element 1: Being Generative—Generosity of Spirit

Element 2: Being the Space of Possibilities—Being Present

Element 3: Being Strategically Aware—Operating from a Place of Heightened *Awareness*

TEN

Being Generative

L eaders are in their highest, most glorious state when they are being generative. The word *generative* may be unfamiliar to many people. The quality of generative energy is something conscious leaders have always sought in their work and life.

I have always adored the word *generative*. There's a certain energy that goes with this word that delights and inspires me. When I refer to the word, I am not only talking about the capacity to produce and create, which is what most people think *generative* refers to. In my view, *being generative* is the essence of who we are. It is the power, potency, and ability to change and transform anything to become something greater than what has been. It's dynamic; it melds our unique skills into an integrated whole.

Generative is the way you feel in those moments when everything is expansive and dynamic, when you are being vibrant and gracious. There is a certain energy and graciousness that goes with this. Gary

Douglas says, "Graciousness is the ability to walk through life without creating waves while leaving behind a sprinkling of cosmic dust of possibility and consciousness."

When you are gracious and choose to create a reality based on infinite choice and infinite possibility, you have a reality that is bigger than anything you could ever imagine right now. When you have generative energy, you have the level of presence and awareness that puts forth energy that generates.

The U.K. billionaire entrepreneur Sir Richard Branson illustrates what it is like to be generative. He epitomizes the energy, space, and consciousness of *being gracious and generative*. He doesn't create anything from control, force, and effort. Every time Branson puts his energy into something, a different possibility and a new door begins to open.

I love how Virgin Atlantic got started. In 1984, Branson was in his late twenties and was going from Puerto Rico to the Virgin Islands to meet his girlfriend. At the airport, his final flight to the Virgin Islands was canceled because the airline didn't have enough passengers to warrant the flight. Rather than waiting for the next available flight, he hired a plane, borrowed a blackboard, and wrote on it "Virgin Airlines" and "$39 one way to BVI." He then went out and rounded up all the passengers who had been bumped and filled up his first plane.

After that, Branson realized he was fed up with airlines that didn't care about their passengers. He wanted to do something about it. A phone call to Boeing to find out if they had any 747s for sale and an airline was born. "We just made it that much more special than all the other airlines we were competing with," Branson says. Three decades after its launch, Virgin Atlantic is the second-largest U.K. carrier. How was he able to do this?

Because Branson creates and generates from a different possibility and a different reality. He is willing to be the generative energy, space, and consciousness—the voice of all possibilities. It's an energy. It's about what he *can* be. He is willing to be and do anything to create a greater possibility. Since Branson is willing to *be* totally different, he can *have* totally different.

He says, "Entrepreneurs must be ready to act on new business opportunities no matter where you are or what you're doing."

Branson shows that it is truly possible to create new and different possibilities from nothing—*if* we are willing to be generative and look for the change that we can create. Most important, Branson was able to step into different possibilities with his business when he was willing to let go of the necessity of making anything stable in his life. He was willing to change anything in a heartbeat.

That meant staying nimble as his airline was first getting off the ground. When Virgin Atlantic was trying to establish itself in the 1990s, British Airways ran what became known as the "dirty tricks" campaign. Virgin Atlantic had only four planes flying, and British Airways went to extraordinary lengths to put Virgin out of business. British Airways had a team of people illegally accessing Virgin Atlantic's computer information and ringing up the passengers and pretending that they were from Virgin, telling them that flights were canceled and switching them onto BA.

Virgin took British Airways to court and won $945,000 in damages, the largest libel settlement in U.K. history. Branson chose to invest the money back into his Virgin Atlantic team. "It was Christmas time," he says. The settlement from British Airways became known as the BA Christmas bonus. Branson distributed it to all Virgin Atlantic staff equally.

Branson is a wonderful example of how to become a source of generative energy in our lives and in the world. He is willing to have a reality so different from everybody else's that he could stand alone, all by himself, and have no point of view. It's not creating separation, however; it's actually being aware of this generative capacity you have that enables you to solidify things into existence.

When you can see *being generative* for what it is, you never eliminate the awareness of possibilities that you could harvest and engender in the world. What if who you can be is greater than where you are right now? What if you can become a powerful agent of change in the world when you acknowledge, claim, and own your generative capacity?

Every one of us has enormous power to generate different possibilities in a positive way. In this interconnected universe, embodying your capacity to be generative means that a shift in your awareness can simultaneously reverberate into the widest global environment to subtly engage and transform everyone.

Being generative is the ability to be or do anything and is therefore the willingness to receive anything. It doesn't require any particular belief or action. As a leader, when you are willing to be totally generative and don't put up a barrier to anything, you get to receive all information and be aware of everything. You are always aware of the energy around you and you choose from what is going to expand your business and your own life. This capacity is what sets conscious leaders apart.

When you are being the energy of a generative, conscious life, you have the ability to readjust every choice you make. No choice is solid or fixed in place. You are aware of what has to be dealt with and what doesn't.

One of the reasons that many business leaders never truly become conscious is they simply cannot get their head around this essential principle of *being generative*. They cannot fathom the basic truth of the universe that everything is connected and that things exist through their relationships with one another.

The conscious leaders who acknowledge their generative energy and power are willing to reach for different possibilities no matter the circumstance. It is only when we reach for it that we find it. Branson says that it is up to all of us to be the innovation we want to see in our businesses. You can't expect people to be innovative if you are not willing to be that yourself. There is no place for judgment of failures nor complacency with success. In the case of Branson, this level of awareness created a global empire that breaks all the traditional rules of business success while having a major impact on people's lives and the entire business world.

Generative always has a sense of generosity of spirit with it.

For a conscious leader, there is no more important energy than *generosity of spirit*. It is the natural element in each of us that is intangible and undefinable. Generosity of spirit is a way of being in your life and in the world. It's about living your life with a sense of joyful generation and wishing well for all. The opposite is penurious—unkind, selfish, stingy, miserly, poverty stricken.

Generosity of spirit is one of the key things that will create more possibilities in your life. If you're not willing to have generosity of spirit, could it be that you are believing in judgment, scarcity, and lack? If business leaders don't have a sense of generosity—if they are not *willing* to have generosity of spirit—they will never truly be generative. In my view, one of the reasons that Richard Branson is so generative and has so much influence is because of his buoyant generosity of spirit.

In this reality, including the business arena, generosity of spirit is a poorly understood idea. Often, its definition is limited to the bounds of social enterprises, philanthropy, or charitable organizations. Few leaders openly embrace it as a foundational tenet for their leadership philosophy. Yet the leaders who have embraced it have enjoyed lasting success.

Ask a group of people what the term generosity of spirit means, and you will get answers such as *kind-hearted, expressing goodwill, charitable, altruistic, philanthropic, unselfish, generous,* and *humanitarian.* The idea of generosity of spirit in business is sometimes confused with concepts used extensively today such as corporate social responsibility (CSR).

But generosity of spirit isn't about being a philanthropist or a humanitarian. It's not about being altruistic. There's nothing lofty about it. It has nothing to do with self-important concepts. What would it be like in your world if you had the generosity of spirit that allowed you to give without ever expecting anything in return? Generosity of spirit is kindness. It is not generosity of money. For example, making a difference and helping others have been integrated in everything Richard Branson does. He functions from *what could I do that would change the world*—not *what could I do to make more money.* He is always pushing the status quo with the idea of making a difference and being the change, along with making work as fun as play, making great products, and providing great services. He is very aware of what he wants to create in the world.

Branson is interested more in what he can create than in the money he gets from the creation. In other words, he does things not because of the money but because of what might be created. Nothing matters more to him than his capacity to be generative, to engender new and different possibilities. The key to his success is simple: his choice to create himself as the source for creating a different world. He is willing to function at a bigger level than anybody else around him.

Branson is an amazing demonstration of a conscious business leader that has achieved phenomenal success and is also making a positive contribution to society and the world. He has created space for greater possibilities by establishing clear conscious leadership, generosity of spirit, and integrating conscious business practices across all of his business endeavors.

What if you were willing to be that level of generosity of spirit in life? What could you create as your reality? Ask, "What can I be today that will create that space?" You CAN be the choice for a different possibility in this world.

———

There is no greater thing you can do with your life and your work than follow your passions in a way that serves the world and you.

—RICHARD BRANSON

———

ELEVEN

Be the Space of Possibilities

Another radical idea that you can embrace to truly become a conscious leader is simply choosing to be *the space of possibilities*. People who achieve remarkable achievement in life are often those who choose to embody and be the space of possibilities. Nelson Mandela once observed, "It always seems impossible until it's done." This is a wonderful analogy regarding the space of possibilities.

The ability to be the space of possibilities has greater applicability when it comes to living and creating our life with conscious awareness. One of the greatest challenges I see with my clients and mentees is that they are focusing on the problems instead of the possibilities. Too many people are forever focused on trying to avoid problems instead of creating from infinite possibilities. Meanwhile, they drift into creating mediocre lives. They are not willing to be and do anything to create a greater possibility; they are not choosing to be the space of possibilities.

Being the space of possibilities is the ability to be present in your life in every moment, without judgment of you or anyone else. You have connection to everything and everyone. You are totally in the moment and able to see clearly what is in front of you. Nothing is more exciting than having awareness—unexpectedly and without effort—of different possibilities.

Being the space of possibilities is where you choose from possibility, where you create from possibility, and where you have infinite possibility. You are unfettered by thoughts, feelings, emotions, fantasies, and past reference points. You're living life at a different level.

A great example is Audrey Hepburn, the first actress to win a Golden Globe, an Academy Award, and a BAFTA for a single performance. Growing up, she had her fair share of hardships and failures. Days after her 11th birthday, Hitler's army stormed into her town in Holland. Nazi occupation remained until liberation came on her 16th birthday. She lived through scarcity and treachery during this time, losing friends, uncles, and almost both brothers. But no matter what life threw her way, Hepburn never failed to forget that life itself was a beautiful opportunity. She saw the world with a different eye. She saw the possibility.

Hepburn suffered greatly during World War II from malnourishment, anemia, and odema (swelling of the legs), yet she retained a strong sense of who she wanted to be in the world. She was secure in her merit and ability and always sustained a sense of wonder about life and the world. The cards she was dealt did not stop her from living life with an open gratefulness and a total willingness to receive without judgment.

She was once a young, unknown woman who dreamed of becoming a ballet dancer. As the story goes, Hepburn asked her teacher, Marie Rambert, "Do you think I could become a prima ballerina?" Rambert answered honestly: "No, Audrey, I don't." She went on to explain how she was one of the best, most dedicated students, but she was too tall to dance with a male dancer. Despite the disappointment, Hepburn didn't let this limit her. She asked, in her own way, "What else is possible?" She knew she was going to get something better. Her life became a constant state of creating.

She realized that she could not be a prima ballerina according to this reality, yet she still chose to be everything she was regardless of other people's points of view. She never judged what was "wrong" about her. Most people would have stopped creating, but Hepburn didn't. She committed to having a life that worked for her whether anybody else could see it or not. She once told a reporter, "I have learnt how to live . . . how to be in the world and of the world, and not just to stand aside and watch."

Unceasingly, she functioned from the space of what would create the greatest future possibilities. Throughout her life, people kept telling her, "What you want is just not possible." Yet Hepburn refused to live her life by other people's points of view; she refused to be and do what others said was right for her. She often said, "Nothing is impossible. The word itself says 'I'm possible'!"

Hepburn had an instinct for what worked for her and what didn't. She revealed that when you are willing to own that *you are a gift*, when you are able to acknowledge *what you are capable of*, you receive possibilities you didn't know you had. You perceive choices and possibilities you never knew could be available to you.

Hepburn did not live any part of her life according to somebody else's point of view. The way she created her reality was impressive and formidable. Whether anybody else agreed with her or liked what she was doing was irrelevant. Early in her career, she was doing twenty-one shows a week in London's West End—*choosing* to be what was going to create the most for her. Her willingness to be the gift and own her power and potency impelled critics to single her out time and time again.

She created her life from the space of possibility, so everything fell into place in a way that seemed auspicious. She was willing to be, do, have, create, and generate anything in order to have her life. Her commitment to herself and her life was powerful; she was willing to create her life from the space of possibility, not from the space of conclusion. Most important, she was willing to go beyond the limitations of this reality. A famous quote from her encapsulates this way of being:

"I probably hold the distinction of being one movie star who, by all laws of logic, should never have made it. At each stage of my career, I lacked the experience. I was asked to act when I couldn't act. I was asked to sing Funny Face when I couldn't sing, and dance with Fred Astaire when I couldn't dance—and do all kinds of things I wasn't prepared for. Then I tried like mad to cope with it. I decided, very early on, just to accept life unconditionally; I never expected it to do anything special for me, yet I seemed to accomplish far more than I had ever hoped. Most of the time it just appeared to me without my ever seeking it."

Her original personal style was an example of her commitment to a life that worked for her whether anybody else liked it or not. She showed a good deal of tenacity toward creating her life beyond the limitations of this reality. She believed in choice and possibilities and never allowed herself to give in to adversity. She always looked at what else she could do, what else she could be, what else she could create, and what else she could generate. She said, "In life, there will always be things you don't think you can do, but as long as you give it a good go and push yourself like crazy, you'll be fine. Even if you fail, you should try. You might discover that you have talents you didn't know you had."

Too often most of us are limited in what we can achieve in life because we are not choosing to be the space of possibilities. You stand a far better chance of being the power and potency that changes reality if you can cultivate your ability to be the space of possibilities. You have to get to the place where you don't create your limitations as greater and more important than your possibilities.

You have to demand of yourself, "No matter what it takes, I am willing to risk everything to actually choose to be the space of possibilities." You have to choose to be totally vulnerable and totally potent and demand, "No matter what occurs I am going to be that." It's a choice and a demand you have to make of yourself. Every choice creates a change, and every choice creates a new set of possibilities. You've got to commit to having a life that works for you whether anybody else likes it or not.

The space of possibilities exists in the present.

Leaders that excel in being the space of possibility tend to be very skilled at being present. To lead your life and business from the space of possibilities, it is vital that you use the present moment powerfully. When you are willing to be totally present and to be anything and everything, you have no limitation in any respect. Everything is available to you. Being becomes a space where new ideas and innovation are generated from a heightened perception and knowing. When you are being the energy, the space, and the consciousness of you, everything can show up for you, because you can receive everything and reject nothing.

To be present with what is and become aware of what is happening, it is important to pay attention with an open mind. It is essential to set aside your personal preconceptions, prejudices, or biases. Prejudiced people see only what fits those preconceptions and prejudices.

The key thing you must choose if you want to live the life you truly want to lead and to create the business from the space of possibility is to make a genuine choice to do so. What does it mean to make a genuine choice? First, you must be willing to choose you, to be you, to show up as you, and to be the energy that creates everything you would like to have. That's what Audrey Hepburn chose to be throughout her life. She was willing to perceive and receive what was going to work for her. She truly lived from the generative question of *what else is possible* with no fixed point of view.

When my husband Steve and I started our consultancy business Conscious Governance a decade ago, we asked ourselves, "What is possible that we have never even considered?" We became aware that there were so many more possibilities available to us than we realized. We started looking at what was going to work for both of us. What did we desire? What did we wish to create? Instead of preparing our strategy and an outcome from conclusion, projection, or expectation, we primed ourselves to receive whatever came. We fostered our ability to live in the process of creation and generation; we were prepared to act, to go wherever things were going. We refused to listen to naysayers. We chose to look at every possibility no matter what was going on.

We became more curious and interested in the adventure of exploration—to see what else was truly possible—than in our plan or the necessity of getting it right. We became clear that our priority in life is to remain in the present moment and connected to infinite possibilities. The most essential goal of our business is to be a catalyst for change and to different possibilities in the world. Everything else takes care of itself. Beyond business, our No. 1 personal practice is choosing to live in the present moment—to resist projecting into the future or lamenting past mistakes; to feel the real power of infinite choice and infinite possibilities.

People often ask us how to create the structure for a business. We say that there is no fixed form or structure, but that doesn't mean we don't have systems and processes. We created a system that is malleable and changeable, that can be altered and fine-tuned according to the moment. Conscious Governance is a generative organization. We don't have rigid rules; we have flexible processes. We adjust according to the moment and the people in it. This comes from us functioning from question, choice, possibility, and contribution—from being willing to listen to the whispers of possibilities. We are always looking for the possibility. We are always asking, "What is possible that we have not yet considered? What is available that has not been chosen?"

When we ask these types of questions, things start to show up for us in a different way. The more we ask the questions, the more aware we become of the choices and possibilities we have. We have found that, when we ask questions in a nonlinear and infinite way, and if we don't have any preconceived idea or expected outcome about the answer, we set the stage for previously unthinkable leaps of consciousness. When we open up to genuine wonder, we step out of the zone of this reality and into that of infinite possibilities.

We find inspiration all around us. My last book, *Leading from the Edge of Possibility—No More Business as Usual*, was inspired by our work facilitating anti-conscious board directors to see different possibilities. All things become possible when we're willing to be the space of possibilities and have the awareness of all things that are possible.

Albert Einstein is a great example of someone who lived *in* the question. His willingness to ask questions and then perceive, know, be, and receive the energies of the universe was his ticket to total awareness. It gave him access to what was possible, and with his genius he was able to access universal knowledge. He questioned the whole notion of time, proposing that speed would allow us to travel beyond the present. He refused to be constrained by the finite potential of contextual reality. His work and achievements did not come from his cognitive ability but from living in the question. This is where the magic begins.

The most beautiful experience we can have is the mysterious. It is the fundamental emotion that stands at the cradle of true art and true science.

—ALBERT EINSTEIN

What we've found over two decades working with CEOs, boards of directors, and business executives around the world is that the most successful people in any field aren't just lucky. They are the creator source of a different possibility, are somehow responsible for everything that occurs, and made everything in their life actualized the way it did. They are willing to follow whatever possibilities present themselves.

Creating the life and the business that works for you whether anybody else likes it or not takes confidence, boldness, and the discipline to be in the present moment and to tune out negative voices. Being present is an ongoing creative, generative movement. It is the willingness and capacity to move and change easily as circumstances arise right now. When you are being totally present and totally aware, you perceive choices and possibilities you never knew could be available. You are aware of what can and cannot be changed far beyond what is considered possible. You are aware of what must be dealt with and what doesn't have to be dealt with.

The key takeaway is this: If you want to be the space of possibility, you must be willing to be totally present. You must be willing to create a reality that has more possibilities in it.

Here are three questions for you to consider:

- What can I do right now that will generate business today and in the future?

- What can I be and do differently today that will generate the success I desire?

- What else is possible?

Being totally present.

Consciousness is the ability to be present in your life in every moment. Being a conscious leader begins with the simple act of being present in any given moment with no conclusion, no projection, no expectation, and no judgment. It means being present in the moment with what is, simply noticing the way things are, and never expecting anything to be different. Being conscious comes from within.

Being totally present brings tremendous power, because it can open doors to everything you are capable of. Being totally present isn't everything, but it is one thing that can make a difference in your life. Without it, we often feel distracted and overwhelmed.

But what is *being present*, anyway? When you hear these words, what do you think about? I think of *being present* as a generative moment that has no target, no goal, and no purpose. Being present means just being and simply noticing the way things are. Look at nature, for example. The trees, plants, flowers, and animals are just here and now.

Animals know not of the past or the future; they simply are present. Animals move freely, unencumbered with thought about where they should be and how they should be acting. They don't see themselves as good or bad, beautiful or ugly, a hard worker or a freeloader.

They are moving through life freely and playfully, without conclusion, projection, expectation, or judgment.

Watch small children playing and what do you see? They are totally present with what is. They are being, exploring, and moving from activity to activity without judging the situation as right or wrong, good or bad—or hoping it was different. They don't worry about the future and easily forget the past; they play and enjoy every moment for what it is.

We can't truly be present and fully see the beauty of being present if we're too hung up on the past or too focused on the future. Too many business leaders slowly lose their ability to live in the present. With more responsibility comes more to be accountable for, more to worry about, and more to plan for. But we can't completely enjoy the gift of the present if we're filled with remorse, judgment, projection, expectation, and anxiety.

Once you appreciate the splendor of the present—the only reality that is here, in this moment—you aren't immersed in the uncertainty for the future or the deduction from the past. Top athletes are a great example. They understand the power of the present moment better than most. Ask athletes what happens when they are not being present. Ask chess masters what happens when they are not being present. They lose! Being totally present is often the marker between winning and losing.

Researchers who study the brains of athletes have found that elite athletes are not only finely tuned for the physical demands of their particular sport. They also have the ability to be totally present in the moment—an essential skill that brings athletes' talents to light and allows them to compete to the best of their abilities. (https://www. scientificamerican.com/article/understanding-elite-athlete/)

Visual attention is the ability to focus on what is currently relevant to whatever you are doing (whether it be one or multiple things) while ignoring distractions. When athletes expand their ability to be in the present moment, they have an advantage known as "changing the breadth of visual attention." Breadth of attention refers to how many things and how much of the environment you are paying attention to at any one time.

Being present "in the now" is a key sports psychology term that athletes hear often. Coaches say, "Come on, concentrate *now.*" Shifting the breadth of attention is essential in sports.

Tennis players know that being totally present is vital to playing the game at their highest level. The one-point-at-a-time mantra is chanted by every coach and top-ranked player. Great tennis players recognize that if they are to play well during tough matches, they must be present, learn to manage pressure, and deal with expectations. A player on the court must focus on the ball and their opponent while filtering out the crowd. This requires the ability to be totally present and have a broad breadth of attention.

French tennis player Caroline Garcia knows how being totally present can ease pressure and improve performance. When Garcia was playing on her home turf at the 2017 French Open, the expectations were enormous: the last French woman to win the French Open was Mary Pierce in 2000. To add to the pressure was Garcia's collapse at the French Open in 2011. She was leading Maria Sharapova 6-3 4-1 in their second-round match when her game fell apart and she lost the next 11 games in a row to lose the match.

During the 2017 French Open, however, Garcia expanded her capacity to be present and dealt effectively with pressure, staving off Hsieh Su-Wei in her third-round match 6-4 4-6 9-7. Garcia credited the ability to stay present for helping her manage the pressure of the big moment. She affirmed that she was able to play to the best of her abilities when she made a choice to be in the moment with her game instead of searching for outcomes and reaching for expectations. Being present with her game assisted her in blocking out negative thoughts, took the focus off the importance of a match, and allowed her to focus on her tactics and strokes.

Often, particularly during a significant match, players tend to dwell on the errors they made or the points they missed. They focus on what they were doing wrong in a match and end up frustrating themselves even more. Garcia advocates that, in order to play well, players must focus on the present. Players must play in the moment in order to succeed!

Being present with your business is
fundamental to connecting with it

When you are present, your awareness is more expanded. Your expanded zone of awareness enables you to take advantage of opportunities and consciously deal with the problems that trap other people. Successful people live by these words from Leo Tolstoy: "There is only one time that is important—NOW! It is the most important time because it is the only time when we have any power."

In our work with business leaders around the world, we've had the opportunity to observe many organizations and the people who lead them. The most dynamic, effective, and generative leaders we've seen are those who have ability to be present in the moment. They are willing to give up fixed expectations and predetermined outcomes to change and transform on a dime.

Functioning in the present seems to come naturally to Ted Nierenberg, the founder of Dansk International. At every turn, Nierenberg has taken the road less traveled. In 1954, he was out of a job, so he and his wife went to Europe on a shoestring budget. Traveling to unusual

places exposed Nierenberg to new experiences and novel ways of looking at the world. He was able to be in the space of no fixed expectations, where new places could be accessed. Throughout the European
trip he considered what he could be and do differently that would
create a different possibility for him and his wife.

Nierenberg was present in a way that led him to new places and
new possibilities. For example, he visited a museum in Copenhagen
where he saw a set of unique cutleries: hand-forged stainless-steel flat-
ware that combined teak handles and stainless steel, an unusual com-
bination at the time. He began to ask, "What is possible here? What
could I be creating here that I haven't even considered?" He was simply
willing to create a reality that has more possibilities in it.

Nierenberg tracked down the designer Quistgaard and asked him
to manufacture the cutlery, but the designer insisted that the pieces
could only be forged by hand, one piece at a time. Nonetheless, Nierenberg had awareness of something totally different and was willing to
look at different possibilities. Nierenberg invited Quistgaard to look at
his choices from a different point of view, asking the designer to consider creating from possibilities he had never considered. He convinced
Quistgaard that the pieces could be mass-produced, leading to Dansk
International Design's first product, the Fjord line, which has been one
of the firm's enduring bestsellers.

Nierenberg was willing to see different possibilities and create
beyond other people's fixed points of view. Willing to let go of the
preconceived notions of how things ought to be, out of something
that seemed impractical Nierenberg created something accessible for
everyday use. His rise to the top was the result of his ability to be present with what is and his willingness to out-create other people's fixed
points of view and their need to hold things in place.

Shortly after their first meeting, Nierenberg and Quistgaard established the American company Dansk Designs in the garage of Nie-

renberg's New York home. A unique and successful Danish-American collaboration stretched over three decades because Nierenberg was willing to function at a bigger level than anybody else around him.

Nierenberg wanted to improve everyday life with kitchenware that combined aesthetics and functionality. He was determined to provide sleek, clean-line design for everyday use. This required him to open his awareness and mind to all possibilities, to resist any efforts to be pigeonholed, and to refuse to allow pessimism into the way he created his business. The company's motto was "from the kitchen to the dining room table," because its pieces' sleek, clean lines were both functional and beautiful. It was Nierenberg's ability to be totally present, his incredible artisanal knowledge and understanding of the materials, and simple yet refined designs that elevated Dansk to its international status.

Being open to the infinite array of possibilities is one of the key principles that Nierenberg adopted to build his business. He had an amazing capacity to go beyond traditional approaches and views about the kitchenware industry. As the casualization movement spread around the world, Nierenberg continued to explore new ways to create useful and expressive tools for entertaining, cooking, and dining.

Dansk's clean, contemporary lines came to epitomize overall Scandinavian design. Nierenberg's commitment to distinctive design has earned Dansk a place in museum collections around the world. With its Scandinavian modern design ethic, Dansk makes everything Dansk go with everything Dansk, and everything Dansk goes with the way people live today.

Practice being present

Your ability to be present in the moment increases your ability to respond consciously and creatively to unexpected situations. In the current environment, in order to thrive and not just merely survive you must be able to make decisions efficiently, quickly, and strategically. To achieve this, you have to cultivate your ability to move beyond logic and analysis and tap into your awareness in the moment to make choices that create something greater.

If you can truly be present, you will be able to recognize what is proceeding and appearing around you clearly. In that moment, your awareness takes over and directs your attention and responses in a more efficient and resourceful way. You are able to consciously choose what to do and what not to do. You can have a major impact on the expansiveness of your organization and the people affected by the organization.

As a leader, you can be super-effective if you develop the ability to be totally present in the moment, to consciously and effectively deal with uncertainty and risk. It may turn out that in a world of exponential change, you will be the one with the essential skills to rise to the top.

To practice being present is an approach to life and a way of being rather than a set of instructions or rules to be followed by all in the same way. At the heart of being present is the need for personal power and the ability to receive everything without judgment. Being present is practical. It's about being with what is, in the here and now with no resistance, no reaction, no resentment, no conclusion, no projection, no expectation, and no judgment. For me, that is the joy of living.

Leading a business and generating your life from being totally present is where you have no fixed thoughts about how things should be. Rather, you have massive amounts of awareness and receive everything with no point of view. When you lead without a point of view and you ask questions—"What is possible that I have not yet considered?" "What is available that has not been chosen?"—you can perceive the energy of what will be created by a choice.

Here are four keys to being totally present:

1. **Let go of preconceived notions of how things ought to look or be.** "Should" and "shouldn't" are not words you should use. Don't function from labels or definitions, or, at least, do not be attached to them.

2. **Be willing to be with what is and don't look for something to be greater than what is.** Being present is simply about being with what is, right now, in the moment, without judging the situation or hoping it was different.

3. **Stop identifying with your thinking mind.** If you do not make yourself subject to your thoughts, feelings, and emotions, you can be totally present and have total choice and awareness of what is going on around you.

4. **Let go of conclusion, projection, expectation, and judgment.** When you conclude, project, or expect anything, you're separating, judging, and rejecting your awareness. You can never see what's actually true.

TWELVE

Being Strategically Aware

Being strategically aware is everything when it comes to leading a thriving business and living a prosperous life. This may seem esoteric, but I have personally experienced time and again how strategic awareness affects business strategies, leadership, and personal growth.

Indelibly linked to the strategic awareness principle is the fact that far too often people adopt a short-term approach to life and business instead of choosing to be aware of future possibilities. So they drift—without awareness and with no strategy. They stepped away from creation and into limitation.

What is strategic awareness . . . really?

What exactly is strategic awareness? Detecting changes in the external environment on a continual basis and knowing what these changes mean to your business. It takes robust strategic awareness to effectively deal with complexity and decipher the ambiguity to identify trends that are emerging.

Some people do not trust that awareness is real. They won't allow themselves to have ease with the awareness that is available to them. They cut off their awareness in order to live in this reality. They push everything away. For many people, they are not even aware that they are doing it.

The connection between awareness and success is not usually recognized and acknowledged. As a result, we often believe people are successful because of their brainpower and extraordinary talent. In fact, it is their expanded zone of awareness that makes them successful. Their expanded zone of awareness enables them to take advantage of opportunities and consciously deal with the problems that trap other people.

Einstein called awareness a sacred gift and believed that awareness was more important than knowledge. How right he was! A key ingredient to success in business and life is to embrace awareness as your greatest confidante and partner rather than view awareness as superficial or irrelevant. Only by fully embracing your awareness can you step into the fullness of life.

Awareness is an innate gift we all have—we just need to learn to tap into it and trust it. By being in touch with your awareness you are, in turn, being in touch with different possibilities. Einstein said, "Knowledge is limited, whereas awareness embraces the entire world, stimulating progress, giving birth to evolution. It is, strictly speaking, a real factor in scientific research." He added that the rational mind was a faithful servant: "It is paradoxical that in the context of modern life we have begun to worship the servant and defile the gift."

Strategic awareness places equal emphasis on both strategy and awareness. However, strategy and awareness work in very different ways. Awareness without strategy often results in leaders becoming mesmerized by the realm of potential possibility. They bounce from one idea to the next without any plan or strategy for carrying ideas through to actualization.

Awareness of the possibilities is important, but it's not enough. You have to be able to bring the ideas into the world—and a generative strategy allows you to do this. Have you met people who talk on and on about their visions and aspirations yet never seem to create anything? A bunch of amazing ideas without robust strategy does not lead to business success. In fact, many notorious big-business failures stemmed from feeble or faulty strategies.

On the other hand, being strategic without awareness means focusing on how to improve or enhance the organization's current capacity or situation while skipping the question, "What else is possible?" Without awareness, leaders easily become blind to changes and developments that the existing strategy has not considered.

Without awareness, the organization focuses exclusively on their strategy. Leaders are not aware of the changes occurring in the world around them. Other possibilities are not recognized. The existing strategy becomes the "right" way to do things. Being strategic without awareness results in a cognitive bias that is prone to confirm evidence believed to be true.

Strategic awareness is a space where different possibilities, new ideas, and innovation are constantly generated from a heightened awareness and from a space of infinite choice and infinite possibilities. With this strategic awareness, leaders operate beyond the goal of competing to actively seize new and different possibilities. They live in the question and act on the possibility of things—instead of trying to create the way other people do. They make the improbable or the seemingly impossible come about by bringing awareness and resources to things that lie beyond contextual reality and business as usual.

With strategic awareness, you expand your capacity and power to create something beyond other people's reality, something that doesn't match anybody else's reality, and something that is considered astonishing. Strategic awareness enormously enhances the probability of success by ensuring that possibilities get generated into reality.

Strategically aware leaders see that an industry's structural conditions are neither inevitable nor finite. They are able to perceive and find distinctive market positions and sustainable advantages in a multitude of ways. They recognize opportunities and seize them.

Neither awareness nor strategy alone is enough. But when awareness meets strategy, it has potential to change the world. Steve Jobs is a good example of what it means to embody strategic awareness. In our view, his phenomenal success was due to his brilliant capacity for marrying awareness with robust strategies. Every innovative product at Apple started with Jobs's intensity of awareness of new possibilities— and a heavy dose of creative strategies that make the possibilities a reality. Not one of Jobs's ideas would have stood a chance of becoming an innovative product had he not been able to operate from strategic awareness.

At the start of the new millennium, Jobs became aware of the power of the digital technology revolution to evolve PC capability to the next level. He saw beyond the horizon and perceived that the PC was on the threshold of entering the digital lifestyle. He then generated strategies to turn the Mac into a digital hub. As part of this strategy, Apple developed the iLife software program, which allowed people to edit video (iMovie), create podcasts (GarageBand), organize photos (iPhoto), and more. The digital hub strategy allowed Apple to prosper and thrive beyond anyone's imagination. It is the first company in the world to reach a market valuation of $1 trillion.

In the next decade, businesses and individuals must embrace the twin pillars of awareness and strategy. Failure to do so will stifle innovation and different possibilities at a period in history when innovation is vital. The good news is that when you become a strategically aware leader, you become a catalyst for innovation and different possibilities. In the face of ambiguities and complications, conscious leaders play to their strategic awareness and take bold actions as they instigate new opportunities to create value.

Strategic awareness increases proficiency, and proficiency increases the multiple streams of possibilities—more choices, higher returns on investment, new business prospects, new ideas, and a prosperous economy. With strategic awareness you are able to perceive and receive the future that you hadn't considered yet. Creating sustainable futures is about awareness. If you desire to create futures that are sustainable, you have to create from expanded awareness, strategy, and true choice.

Lack of strategic awareness is a recipe for misfortune. Traditional strategic planning is not enough if you are to adapt and thrive in this tumultuous business world; you must also expand your strategic awareness. If you know how to consistently generate new and different possibilities, regardless of your particular enterprise, you have a much greater chance to succeed and generate futures that are sustainable. Otherwise, you may become obsolete.

Strategic awareness is a process—fusing awareness to strategy and incorporating real-world knowledge of industry, global trends, and possible futures. It is the process of accessing non-analytic data and incorporating awareness or inner knowing into the strategic decision-making process. According to the legendary virologist Dr. Jonas Salk, "Awareness will tell the thinking mind where to look next."

Strategic awareness combines the power of awareness with generative strategy.

It is about . . .

1. Being totally aware.

2. Being open to the infinite array of possibilities.

3. Being spontaneous, flexible, adaptive, and responsive.

I. Being totally aware

Awareness is one of the most overlooked capacities we possess. Our modern cultural bias for intellect and analysis doesn't value awareness as highly as it should. For many business executives, the power of awareness seems mysterious. Many people think awareness is something they either have or don't have. But that's not true; it is available to all of us. We all have the ability to tap into this power.

Awareness is an indefinable power in each of us. It affects how we live our life, create our reality, navigate business complexities, and make personal choices. We *can* continuously access our awareness and use it to our advantage. But if we're like most people, we may not realize it's there. When we ignore or disregard our awareness, we are limiting our capacity to achieve success in business and in life.

However successful your current business may be, if you constantly contract your awareness you will not be aware of the choices and possibilities available to you.

To expand your vibration level and become the catalyst for change and transformation, you have to expand your zone of awareness. The zone of awareness is a real psycho-physiological experience that each of us can choose to have right now. It is like a spherical atmosphere, where everything is in constant movement around us. This is the realm of infinite possibility. When you function from an expanded zone of awareness, you start opening the door to creating from a different place—and a different possibility begins to occur.

Awareness is the capacity to know everything. It is a continuous, ever-moving, ever expanding possibility. It is the ability to be totally present in life without judgment of anything that goes on. It is also the willingness to receive in totality the abundance and exuberance of life. With an expanded zone of awareness, you have the power to move beyond logic and analysis and to make choices that are conscious, insightful, and innovative. If you don't expand your zone of awareness, you diminish your potential as a leader. You are apt to blindly steer your business into the future.

Awareness is the place where no point of view is necessary. When you are aware, you have the ability to see and perceive, to know and be—to receive the totality of something without having to come to conclusion. If you are willing to perceive everything without judgment, you have infinite choice.

Awareness isn't just about "trusting your gut." It's a tool to help you make a choice. Former Special Air Service Commando John Taske knows about accessing awareness for decision-making in stressful situations. Taske is famous for surviving a 1996 climb of Mt. Everest that ended in tragedy for others. He attributes his survival to his awareness: He decided to abort his climb just 300 meters shy of the Mt. Everest peak. Unfortunately, others continued—based on their rational minds (all conditions seemed okay)—and perished. Taske had an awareness that things were not okay. This conscious choice was made days earlier as part of his strategy to preserve oxygen and daylight if the climb became delayed. John survived. Tragically, all nine climbers that ignored the strategy perished.

Four keys to expand your awareness:

Be willing to receive everything in life.

1. Be willing to let go of any fixed points of view you might have created.

2. Be willing to let go of conclusion, projection, expectation, assumption, and judgment of any kind.

3. Be willing to stop identifying with your mind, thoughts, feelings, or emotions.

Awareness is seen as not important to business leaders who prefer to align themselves with conventional business models. This is all in an effort to achieve winning outcomes, of course, but most conventional business leaders distrust their awareness and rely solely on empirical evidence as the basis for conducting the business and for their decision-making processes. These leaders tend to be keen to *do* and to *act*; they often feel they don't *need* to access their awareness to be successful.

For years I've been talking about the imperative of awareness in business, and I'm still often asked, "What does being successful in your business have to do with your being aware?" Or, "Why do business leaders need to expand their zone of awareness?" Sometimes I find that people regard "awareness" as another abstruse management theory or New Age principle.

A number of recent scientific studies validate the importance of awareness in business. They show that awareness working in concert with data and well-examined information leads to better decision-making. If you do an online search of awareness and decision-making, there is a multitude of evidence that people can use their awareness to make faster, more accurate, and more confident decisions.

Awareness is a source of new and different possibilities. Your awareness makes a difference in your approach to business and life. With an expanded zone of awareness, you are able to perceive what is going on around you and take action quickly. In contrast, leaders who subscribe to the conventional business-as-usual paradigm tend to be myopic. They focus only on the business close at hand. They tend to have deadly blind spots and miss opportunities.

In the complex, dynamic world of today, it is becoming more and more important in business for decisions to be made quickly. Rapid changes in the business arena cause much uncertainty and put a high premium on spotting or creating changes in the market before others do. Analysis and data are often not available, or they are impractical to employ. Lack of definitive criteria, time and resource constraints, and irregular situations are all instances that limit the feasibility of data. Instead of relying on data that may not even be there, trust your awareness. In these circumstances, awareness is your savior. By using and leveraging your awareness, you can swiftly make effective decisions.

When it comes to relying on data, having too much information can actually be as dangerous as having too little. According to research from Stanford and Princeton psychologists, too much information might actually lead you to make worse choices. Among other problems, information overload can lead to a paralysis of analysis, making it far harder to make the most effective decisions. These are the situations in which our awareness can play a central role.

Business today is jam-packed with ambiguity and change, and we can easily get trapped into destructive, rather than generative, decisions. Even our smallest decisions can have a huge impact on our future positions, but most of us still make these decisions without any overall perspective or the capacity to look at all possibilities.

Many of the world's top movers and shakers are attuned to their awareness and use it to propel their businesses forward. Society-changing individuals like Albert Einstein, Oprah Winfrey, and Richard Branson have an intensity of awareness. They are able to tap into ideas from outside of time and space.

Dr. Jonas Salk, the renowned virologist who discovered the first vaccine against poliomyelitis, has said, "It is always with excitement that I wake up in the morning wondering what my awareness will toss up to me, like gifts from the sea. I work with it and rely on it. It's my partner." Dr. Salk trusted his awareness. He was willing to have total choice and total possibility with no point of view about how it showed up or what it looked like.

Indeed, the ability to access his awareness enabled Dr. Salk to see different possibilities and develop one of the first successful polio vaccines. Until 1955, when Dr. Salk's vaccine was introduced, polio was one of the most frightening public health problems in the world. In his vaccine development, Dr. Salk followed his awareness and challenged prevailing scientific orthodoxy. He was open to the question of what *can* get created instead of concluding what *should* be created. He never came to conclusions and answers.

He was choosing for the possibility even though he had no idea what it looked like. The possibilities were based on his awareness and the energy he could perceive. While most scientists believed that effective vaccines could only be developed with live viruses, Salk developed a "killed-virus" vaccine by growing samples of the virus and then deactivating them, by adding formaldehyde, so that they could no longer reproduce. He never gave up his awareness in order to buy the rightness of this reality.

Dr. Salk was functioning from greater awareness and was willing to be totally different. As the benign strains were injected into the bloodstream, the vaccine tricked the immune system into manufacturing protective antibodies without the need to introduce a weakened form of the virus into healthy patients. Dr. Salk was willing to have that awareness and be that awareness and to create the polio vaccine that was possible beyond this reality. He demonstrated that if we are willing to *be* totally different, we can *have* totally different.

He was willing to create a different reality without needing anyone else to understand, see, or follow what he was doing. Many researchers, such as virologist Albert Sabin, who was developing an oral "live-virus" polio vaccine, called Salk's approach dangerous. Sabin even belittled Salk as "a mere kitchen chemist."

But Dr. Salk was willing to be aware and trust his knowing of what the result would be if he chose to develop a "killed-virus" vaccine. He knew what he wanted to create and where he was going, and he knew when he was going to go for it. He wasn't willing to give himself up for anybody else's point of view.

2. Being open to the infinite array of possibilities

When you are being totally aware, you open to the infinite array of possibilities in your life and your business. Being aware nourishes your sense of deep appreciation and at the same time generates more energy. In some undefinable way, by being totally aware you become more efficient, generative, creative, productive, and energetic. Being more attentive without being distracted by the task in front of you. Not only do you become absorbed and engaged in that moment, you become that moment.

Allowing ourselves to be open to everything sounds easy enough until we think about how much conditioning has taken place in our life and how many of our current thoughts and points of view have been influenced by other people. We are so used to taking a point of view and, in the process, eliminating space and different possibilities. This is where we create a limitation, where we cannot be aware of any other choice, possibility, or contribution.

Being aware does not equal being in control.

Being aware means you have more possibilities than you had previously considered. It doesn't mean you get to have everything you want. Being aware does not equal being in control. Most people misidentify that they can use awareness as a way to control and get everything they desire. They think that if they are functioning from awareness then they get to have whatever they want. This is not true.

Control is always about how to get it right. Being in control is what you use to justify every limitation in your reality and to maintain everything as it currently is without changing anything. It is what you use to make sure you do not change. The need to be in control is the eradication of your awareness—as soon as you have the need to control or think you have to be right, you never allow yourself to have the awareness of whatever else is possible. Control always requires conclusion, projection, expectation, decision, and judgment. The need to be in control is the need to have the right answer.

I'm inspired by Warren Buffet's capacity to function with awareness. For the past thirty years I've been studying Buffet's ways of being and investing. One of his most important insights about investment, business, and leadership is that when you manage your business from awareness you don't have to do control. When you are being totally aware, you don't have to control the way things are generated. As a corollary, not being totally aware means you always try to control what occurs.

Buffet has said, "What an investor needs is the ability to select businesses to invest. Note that word *select*: you don't have to be an expert on every company, or even many. You only have to be able to assess companies within your circle of competence. The size of that circle is not very important; knowing its boundaries, however, is vital."

When choosing to invest in stocks or in businesses, it is essential to never have any conclusions, projections, expectations, separations, judgments, or rejections of any information or data or anyone. One of the reasons Buffett is a renowned investor is because he is always perceiving rather than believing. He is always capable of adjusting according to the moment.

The real secret to Warren Buffett's wealth

The secret to Buffett's wealth is his ability to operate his business from total awareness, which allows him to create his business in a way that gives Berkshire Hathaway enormous strategic advantage. For example, Berkshire's more uncommon cost of leverage is due to its insurance float. (The difference between premiums collected and claims paid out is called insurance float.) Collecting insurance premiums up front and later paying a diversified set of claims is like taking a loan. Buffett's low-cost insurance and reinsurance business have given him a significant advantage in terms of unique access to cheap, term leverage. By using the insurance float as a sort of super-efficient margin account with none of the drawbacks of margin debt, Buffett was able to parlay between 11 and 15 percent compounding results in his equity portfolio, along with reinvested earnings from the operating subsidiaries, into more than 20 percent average annual gains in book value . . . for half a century.

In his 2002 Berkshire Hathaway Shareholder Letter, Buffett wrote, "To begin with, float is money we hold but don't own. In an insurance operation, float arises because premiums are received before losses are paid, an interval that sometimes extends over many years. During that time, the insurer invests the money . . . This pleasant activity typically carries with it a downside: The premiums that an insurer takes in usually do not cover the losses and expenses it eventually must pay. That leaves it running an 'underwriting loss,' which is the cost of float. An insurance business has value if its cost of float over time is less than the cost the company would otherwise incur to obtain funds. But the business is a lemon if its cost of float is higher than market rates for money."

Insurance float has been an enormous contributor to Buffett's success with Berkshire Hathaway. Because premiums received are essentially like loans from policyholders (that only need to be paid back when a claim is made sometime in the future), Buffett has been able to use insurance float as leverage when investing in stocks and private companies, which has a significant, positive impact on the company's return for its shareholders.

When it comes to finance and investment success, you will often find that the difference between success and failure is determined by whether someone is prepared to be a strategically aware business leader. Buffet once famously said, "I am a better investor because I am a businessman, and a better businessman because I am an investor." He's rightly implying that his business shrewdness is part of the reason that Berkshire Hathaway's book value and market value have grown at 20 percent per year since 1965—compared to just 10 percent per year for the S&P 500.

Buffet's ability to move beyond other people's reality is his strategic advantage. The insurance company collects money in the form of premiums; Buffett invests that money and then pays out claims as needed at some future date. He never projects and expects that he knows what's going on. He always looks at what he has to deal with.

At the end of 2016, Berkshire Hathaway's insurance float totaled $91.6 billion. And because Berkshire Hathaway's insurance operations are run at an underwriting profit, the company's insurance float is essentially like a $91.6 billion interest-free loan that Berkshire is actually being *paid* to take. (Buffett says Berkshire earned $28 billion of pre-tax income over fourteen years. In other words, the company was basically paid $2 billion a year to borrow $91.6 billion, which it could then use to invest.)

Buffet has exemplified how, when we are truly functioning with awareness, with great ease we can create financial reality beyond this reality. *Truly functioning with awareness* is where you choose from possibility, where you create from possibility, and where you have infinite possibility. Buffett has been willing to create from what he knows instead of what everybody else projects and expects. He never suppresses his awareness in order to function and live by the projections and expectations of others.

The key point here is that *expanded awareness* is an open-ended universe in which anything becomes possible, everything is available, and the choices you make determine how you are willing to be with yourself and everybody around you. You get to be aware of everything in totality. New and different possibilities show up when you allow yourself to be in the natural flow of infinite choice and infinite possibilities and to have the ease of that.

Awareness is the place where being in control isn't necessary. When you are aware, you have the ability to see and perceive, to know and be, and to receive the totality of something without coming to conclusion.

Total awareness does not give you the right answer

This reality teaches you to come up with the "right" conclusion, the "right" answer. This is not awareness. Coming to the "right" conclusion or answer does not allow you to flow with the energy, choices, or possibilities. If you identify awareness itself as the "right" solution, answer, or conclusion, it is no longer awareness.

Nobody has it right. People only think they do. Even Warren Buffett doesn't always have it right. When you think you have it right, all you're doing is setting yourself up to lose. We all inevitably make mistakes. The great power is to see different possibilities in every mistake and slipup. Buffett believes you can do well if you are willing to see possibilities in every setback. Every time he faces setback he asks, "Okay, what's next? What else is possible?"

The biggest determination of how successful you will be as a conscious leader is how you deal with setbacks and how you treat adversity. If you have no points of view and no projections, expectations, separations, judgments, or rejections, you can be aware of everything and change pretty much anything. But as long as you're making projections and creating expectations, you can never see what's actually true. You will be at the effect of setbacks.

Buffett learned early on that it is important to look at the big picture, the future of a business—not merely the day-to-day details of the market. His genius is in his ability to operate from expanded awareness and in his agility in understanding where value is and swiftly doing something about it. His gift is being able to move ahead of the crowd. He has the willingness to see what is available to him in every moment.

Buffett is clearly one of the greatest investors of all time. He has a net worth of $82 billion, according to *Forbes*, which makes him one of the richest people on the planet. Yet, despite his generative energy and dynamic capacity to function with awareness, and, of course, his remarkable success, there have been slipups over the years. Unlike some executives who try to pass the blame to an underling, Buffett owns his errors and assumes full responsibility when he fails to deliver to shareholders.

His first slipup was in buying control of Berkshire Hathaway. It was an epic failure; he called it a "$200 billion-dollar blunder." He made this mistake because he had decided what the investment was going to be instead of being in the question, "What is the possibility here?" Buffett first invested in Berkshire Hathaway in 1962, when it was a failing textile company, from the conclusion of *what should be created*. He wasn't being in the question, "What is this going to create?"

When Buffett anticipated that Berkshire Hathaway had great potential as a textile company, he had already concluded what the potential was. He wasn't in the question, "How is this going to work out?" He had decided the stock was a great buy and he would make a big profit when more mills closed. So he loaded up on the stock. (Later, the firm tried to cheat Buffett out of money . . . long story.) He admitted that he was looking for a conclusion rather than asking a question that would create a possibility he had never considered. Buffett committed a major amount of money to a terrible business and then tried to sell it, but no one would buy. The textile mill continued to disintegrate, and it eventually shut down.

Though Buffett knew that, as a business, textile manufacturing was unpromising, he looked for the potential amount of money he could make—not the *possibility* of it. He was tempted to buy because the price looked cheap. Stock purchases of that kind had been rewarding in his early years, but by the time Berkshire came along in 1965 that strategy was not ideal. Understanding his mistake, Buffett admitted that his decision to buy Berkshire Hathaway was a terrible one. He estimated this slipup to have cost him $200 billion.

Having learned from his own mistakes, Buffet advises, "Should you find yourself in a chronically leaking boat, energy devoted to changing vessels is likely to be more productive than energy devoted to patching leaks . . . The most important thing to do if you find yourself in a hole is to stop digging."

As successful as he has become, Buffett made a series of ineffective choices earlier in his career. These compelled him to look at the reality he had available but had never chosen. Through a costly lesson learned, he recognized that behind every problem is a possibility. He learned to create more regardless of anybody else's point of view: "I always knew I was going to be rich," he has said. "I don't think I ever doubted it for a minute." Buffett knew all along that he could create a different reality without needing anyone else to understand, see, or follow what he was doing. He was and is willing to function at a bigger level than anybody else around him.

The way he deals with setbacks is deeply admirable. What separates Buffet from the average investor is a total and absolute commitment when things do not go as intended. He simply resolves to get back on the horse and never give up. He is irrepressible and tenacious. Rather than giving up and allowing Berkshire Hathaway to fail, he diversified the business into one of the greatest success stories of the century. His company has become so successful because of Buffett's awareness of different possibilities: He reinvests the profits and cash flows of the original textile operation in highly profitable ways.

Buffett didn't hide from this huge error. To the contrary, he came right out and admitted the mistakes he had made. The way he chooses to be with his business and investment strategy serves as a reminder that whatever you have as your investment strategy, there will be circumstances when you experience downturns and adverse results. Mistakes and failure are simply a part of the process. Buffett's investment slipups are encouraging because they highlight that being totally aware does not equal being in control. It's a great insight into how even the greatest investors cannot control every result to get everything they want.

Success does not follow a straight line, and even the greatest investors still make many slipups. Buffett has proven that we must not choose to invest based on the money, but to invest from being aware of what it is going to create. It is about being the question and the energy to create a different possibility, as well as a willingness to change, to never give up, to never give in, and to never quit.

He kept the Berkshire Hathaway name as a reminder that, with investments, everything has to be about possibility, never about problem. Berkshire Hathaway evolved from a textile manufacturer into a holding company now worth over $300 billion. Berkshire now owns companies like See's Candy Shops, the *Buffalo News*, and World Book International, as well as major positions in companies such as American Express, Disney, Coca-Cola, Gannett, Gillette, and the Washington Post Company. It also is a major insurer that includes GEICO Corporation in its holdings. At the 2017 annual shareholder meeting, investors were greeted with $44.9 billion in profits. And the company is swimming in cash, with $116 billion in retained cash and equivalents.

Who Buffett chooses to be inspires me to see that I have infinite possibility to choose success. To access those possibilities, I have to make the demand of myself to never give up, never give in, and never quit. I know now that no matter what transpires in my life and in my business, if I keep going and creating and generating . . . ultimately I will be successful.

Buffett prides himself on making swift, conscious, and well-informed choices, never waiting for anybody or anything to come to fruition. He simply goes out and creates, and things come to fruition as they do. He deems any unnecessary dilly-dallying as "thumb sucking." Do your research thoroughly, well in advance. Gather all the necessary information and then act decisively. Say no if you have to.

When you choose to operate from expanded awareness without conclusion, projection, expectation, or judgment, you can accomplish anything with ease. With awareness you perceive new and different possibilities that allow you to generate and create beyond anything you ever knew was possible. But remember that it doesn't give you the right way or the right answer. Every answer is the eradication of your awareness. As soon as you think you have the answer or have it right, you will never allow yourself to have the awareness of what else is possible. What if you never had to be right?

Buffett likes to say that there are no called strikes in investing. Strikes occur only when you swing and miss. When you're at bat, don't concern yourself with every pitch, nor should you regret good pitches that you didn't swing at. In other words, you don't have to have an opinion about every stock or other investment opportunity, nor should you feel badly if a stock you didn't pick goes up dramatically.

Total awareness does not give you the right answer or a comfortable reality. Sometimes you have to be with things that are uncomfortable. In fact, you will often be uncomfortable, because, really, we don't have any control. Allowing yourself to be with things that are uncomfortable is vital. Some people think that with expanded awareness they will get clarity and comfort about their problem or the situation they have to deal with. They are looking for clarity—which means they've already decided what it is they're looking for. And when they don't get the answer they want, they go into judgment and create doubt, not possibility. Functioning from "I've got to get the right answer" is certainly not about being aware of what is possible.

Total awareness is about opening to the choice of new possibility and to the question of what can get created instead of the conclusion of what should be created. Choosing stocks and companies to invest in gets a lot easier when you let your awareness guide you. It is about being aware of how something will actually work for you. By being the questions—"What is it going to create? What possibilities are available here that I haven't yet considered?"—you act from that space and receive the contribution of a different possibility, a different choice.

Never give up, never give in, and never quit. Buffett lives this way. He makes sure that he is in a constant state of creation. He never gives up his creation, he never gives up what's great about him, and he never gives up what's possible for him.

3. Being Spontaneous, Flexible, Adaptable, Responsive

Becoming an aware leader is worth your effort, because awareness truly impacts every aspect of your life. It doesn't matter whether you're an entrepreneur, a CEO of a major corporation, a small businessperson, a teacher, or a parent. A high level of awareness will improve your life.

The pressure to sustain a business in our wildly chaotic and frantic marketplace falls on the individual leader. Today's leaders must be more strategic, more aware, and more flexible—and have stronger decision-making capability. An expanded zone of awareness allows you to see different possibilities, recognize different courses of action, and invest in possible futures. It is not about the ability to *predict* the future; it is the capacity to *be present* with all things at all times, without judgment of anything that goes on.

Imagine a life brimming with spontaneity, flexibility, and suppleness. See yourself leading effortlessly, poised and ready for any adventure. Hear yourself presenting and speaking at a meeting without a script. Feel a sense of ease with any obstacle, able to change and transform on a dime.

Being spontaneous, flexible, adaptable, and responsive are skills that can be learned. It is a way of being that emphasizes a flexible mind, open to all possibilities. It is not a scientific method; everything in nature operates this way. It is certainly not a prescription for an aimless or careless approach to life. We all know some leaders who flaunt spontaneity as the virtue. They use "going with the flow" to justify selfish conduct.

To be spontaneous, flexible, adaptable, and responsive, it is essential that you use your awareness adeptly. Instead of preparing a certain outcome, ready yourself for whatever may come. Open your awareness, be willing to receive it all with no judgment, and know that there's a different possibility available. If you're going to create futures that are sustainable, you must choose to make the most of your awareness, stop following business-as-usual paradigms, and audaciously renounce the status quo. Do not take on the limited points of view that other people buy into, and refuse to let bureaucracy stifle your awareness. Do not allow yourself to operate within the limitations of this reality or be bound by what is.

Inability to be spontaneous, flexible, adaptable, and responsive can limit, inhibit, and obstruct your awareness of what's possible for you as a leader—and what's possible for your business and the planet. The demise of Blockbuster is an example of this inability. This company's senior leaders were closed off to other possibilities. They refused to see the implications of the potentially disruptive technology and service that Netflix represented; they ignored what was happening around them. They were stuck in the past where the video rental business had been hugely profitable; it had grown and became very successful organically. They settled on the original strategy that had brought them millions of dollars of success. They believed in their superior marketing advantage as the largest video rental company in the world. They viewed themselves as the leaders in the sector. Because they held on to this established point of view, they refused to see anything that did not support this view of their leadership.

Blockbuster's leadership team was enamored with their original business model, believing in it so much that they were unable to be spontaneous, flexible, adaptable, and responsive. They concluded from the rightness of their point of view and refused to see different choices and different possibilities as they arose. Deciding that any point of view is right sets the limitation in motion and keeps it moving in only that direction. Blockbuster assumed that brick-and-mortar video rental stores were, and ever would be, the most preferred method of movie and video consumption. They couldn't see other possibilities because they had shut them out of their awareness with their fixed point of view.

Blockbuster lost their huge customer base due to unconscious leadership. When the whirlwinds of change swept through the movie and video industry, Blockbuster stuck to their guns. They never asked, "What possibility do we have here that we have never considered?" The greatest form of unconscious leadership is the unwillingness to change due to the rightness of a fixed point of view—exactly what Blockbuster did. Their unwillingness to change spilled over into every business decision they made, preventing them from acting early and competently.

Blockbuster's failure reinforces the fact that when leaders operate their business from a fixed point of view and conclusion, nothing that does not match their reality can even come into their awareness. They lack total choice and couldn't see the opportunity right in front of them. In 2000, the founder of Netflix, Reed Hastings, flew to Dallas to propose a business deal to Blockbuster CEO John Antioco and his leadership team. Hastings got laughed out of the room. Blockbuster went bankrupt in 2010; Netflix is now a $28 billion company.

Blockbuster's team was so fixed and adamant about what they already knew and believed to be true that they completely limited themselves to one way of doing things. The result? Their inability to see what was truly possible. The conclusions that Antioco and his team had already formed about the business and the future of video totally obstructed their ability to look at the whispers of what might be happening—these networks of unseen connections—and using these to their advantage.

The biggest risk today, in our hyper-changing world, is staying with old paradigms. Blockbuster could have started delivering DVDs or could have just bought Netflix to ensure its longevity in the market. It did none of that, and the rest is history. Not adjusting to new environments—being unaware of other possibilities—accounts for most business failures. When you perceive everything that is possible in the universe, it changes your capacity to choose.

Strategic Awareness at work!

Strategic awareness is not a new concept, yet it has been discounted, ignored, and overlooked by conventional business people because it works in ways that are mysterious to their linear, analytic minds. Strategic awareness begins with awareness, which we define as the ability to know without the use of rational thought processes or direct cognition. It is the capacity to know without words and to perceive the truth without explanation, cognitive interpretation, reasoning, or justification.

To have confidence in making choices from awareness, you have to trust that the gift of awareness is a natural, innate capacity within you. You must eliminate any limiting beliefs about what you think is possible. That is, you must believe it is truly possible to access your awareness. You have to suspend your disbelief. If you don't believe in and value your awareness, you won't be able to overcome any limiting beliefs and use your awareness to its fullest.

Accessing your awareness is probably not a common practice for you—it isn't for most people—and it might not even be something that you have even considered. If you choose to become a conscious leader, you must get to the place where you are willing to receive your awareness, the insight that arises from it, and then apply it in your life and business. Learning to receive your awareness is the willingness to allow things to come to you, whether you understand it or not, and with no point of view about how it shows up or what it looks like when it shows up. It's the willingness to receive the information that is available. Accessing your awareness is about being willing to receive it.

You can expand your awareness whenever you choose. It involves a full engagement in the present moment—a willingness to be open to whatever comes up and whatever you perceive in the moment. This is sometimes difficult, because you have to be willing to let go of your old way of relying on your logical and analytical ability. You have to be willing to let go of the step-by-step, linear way of being. Awareness can take you places logic and analytical ability never will. And when you integrate your awareness with logic and analytical ability, you'll make even more conscious choices.

Most of us have been trained to be logical and come up with the right conclusion and the right answer. This is not functioning from awareness. How much logic are you using to create the lack of awareness you are choosing? When you try to work out the right answer, you go into your logical mind. We tend to be so fixed and adamant about what we already know and believe to be true, which greatly limits our power.

Many of us constantly refer to past reference points because of our need for certainty. This need is fundamentally about survival and avoiding discomfort. It's a universal need that drives our choices and conduct. Continuous discomfort for most people means persistent anxiety, and that eventually leads to breakdown. Most of us need to feel certain that we can avoid discomfort and, ideally, find some security and protection in our lives. For most people, it's frightening to step into the unknown. It's distressing for them to have discomfort. And it can be overwhelmingly difficult to have that sense of uncertainty about what lies ahead. So, we hang on to the past. Because even if it's steeped in terrible experiences, it's what we are familiar with and what we feel certain about.

Making decisions solely from past reference points because of your need for certainty is a formula destined to embed mediocrity in your life and business. Letting go of past reference points is not always easy. For many leaders, making decisions and moving forward comes only after evaluation, comparison, analyzing, and planning, all of which they think they must do to make their decision-making process valid. Only when they are convinced, when they are sure that they've got "all of their ducks in a row," do they proceed. And this is what becomes the driving force behind everything they do and determines the direction of their lives.

It helps to be analytical, smart, and coherent, but what makes people like Muhammad Yunus, Richard Branson, and Warren Buffett great business leaders is not their indisputable intellect but their high level of awareness. Although logic is indispensable in business practice, it can lead you astray when it is not integrated with awareness. Why? Logic is typically based on past reference points and objectives. You reach conclusions based on what you already know. And once you have an answer, that's the sum total of what can show up for you.

If you put too much emphasis on past experiences, you focus only on the potential of what could be created. When you pay too much attention to potential, you can block your capacity to access your awareness. Potential is what you think is going to happen or what can happen based on something else happening. Potential is always a conclusion. If you say, "This new product has great potential," you have already concluded what the potential is. You have decided and concluded its impending prospect. When you make your decision based on the potential and follow that up with a fixed point of view about that potential, no new possibilities can be created.

It's much easier for most of us to make decisions based on fact and past reference points than with our awareness. But when we make decisions based on reference points, we tend to adhere to our past practices whether they work or not. Whenever you are sticking to your past practices, you are disengaging, judging, and rejecting anything that would give you awareness. In fact, you're eliminating your awareness, which can lead to seriously adverse outcomes. Blockbuster, Kodak, Polaroid, Tower Records, and Borders all made this sort of mistake. They were guilty of seeing the future as a version of their past success rather than accepting that the digital revolution would totally change and restructure their industries. These companies couldn't perceive or receive any other information that didn't fit their fixed point of view.

True strategic awareness is about choosing your possibilities. It's about opening to the choice of new possibility and to the question of what can get created instead of the conclusion of what should be created.

Harness the power of your strategic awareness

If you wish to make your business take off from wherever it is right now, you must harness the power of your strategic awareness. Analysis alone will never be adequate. Most people doubt their awareness and rely solely on empirical evidence as the basis for their decision-making processes. We believe that empirical evidence is useful—but only in a limited way. It is designed to ensure one's survival. It is about continued existence. Relying on empirical evidence may keep you in business, but it won't allow you to operate on the edge of what is possible. In short, it keeps you from thriving and flourishing.

In my quest to generate change and transformation in the world, I studied business leaders who have generated affirmative change in the world. My exploration confirms that leaders who generate phenomenal success as well as transformational change tend to operate with a high level of strategic awareness.

Steve Jobs illustrates this. Jobs was radically creative and lived his life by his reality, not somebody else's. He functioned from the question, "What possibility do I have that I have never considered?" He encouraged wild and bold runaway thoughts and constantly asked, "What else can we choose beyond this?" He allowed his team to explore and play around to see what else was possible. This led to breakthroughs as much as it did dead ends. Jobs said, "The trick is to know which is which." He never came to conclusions and answers; he just trusted his awareness and knew when to say no.

He was spontaneous, flexible, adaptable, and responsive. At the same time, he was extremely meticulous about creativity and awareness. He was also willing to have total choice and total possibility—with no point of view about how his choice might show up or what it looked like when it showed up.

Jobs saw what it was he wanted to create in the world. He wanted to create easy-to-use technology for the widest possible audience and put computers into the hands of everyday people. It's not just money he got to create; he wished to create a change in the world. Jobs fully embraced the notion that every choice creates a change and every choice creates a new set of possibilities. He always operated beyond traditional thinking, discovering what the new and different possibilities were. He then chose from possibilities. He saw the infinite choice and infinite possibilities in every setting, and he never came to a conclusion that would limit those possibilities.

The ability to operate with strategic awareness means attaining a level of awareness where previously inconceivable things are available. "That was the essence of Jobs's unique genius," wrote the *Wall Street Journal.* "Understanding that absence defines presence; that the only path to the great new things of the future was the merciless elimination of the good old things of the past."

When you are willing to function from expanded awareness and follow your curiosity, you are so powerful that nobody can stop you. You follow whatever possibilities present themselves.

It was Jobs's expanded awareness that made the iPhone possible. Apple had spent huge amounts of time and money developing a prototype tablet (precursor to the iPad). One day, after a presentation by some of the technical people on progress with the tablet, Jobs realized that what they had learned from this research was going to have a greater impact on society through developing a phone rather than the tablets they were researching. He shelved all research on the tablets, redirected everyone to develop the iPhone, and only after the iPhone had been released and become such an iconic feature in our lives did he go back to developing and releasing the tablets.

Even though he had no idea what it would ultimately look like, Jobs was choosing for the possibility when he directed his team to develop the iPhone rather than tablets. He was choosing for the possibilities based on the energy he could perceive. He was willing to truly choose for the possibility by following his awareness and asking, "What are the possibilities that no one has ever even considered?" It's hard to overstate the gamble Jobs took when he unveiled the iPhone in January 2007. Not only was he introducing a new kind of phone—something Apple had never made before—he was doing so with a prototype that barely worked.

Even though the iPhone wouldn't go on sale for another six months, he wanted the world to want one right then. In truth, the list of things that still needed to be done was enormous. A production line had yet to be set up. Only about a hundred iPhones even existed, all of them of varying quality. Some had noticeable gaps between the screen and the plastic edge; others had scuff marks on the screen. And the software that ran the phone was full of bugs. Yet his willingness to choose for the possibility and follow his awareness of what could be set off an entire rethinking of how humans interact with machines.

Indeed, Jobs and Apple have had a string of hits greater than any other innovative company in modern times: iMac, iPod, iTunes Store, Apple Stores, MacBook, iPhone, iPad, App Store—not to mention every Pixar film. They have created products that match and gratify people's dream of a better life.

Jobs made decisions based on his awareness of customers' needs, hopes, and dreams. Apple is tremendously successful and generative because they are aware of the needs and desires of their core customers. Strategic awareness was integral to Jobs's way of doing business. He behaved as if the normal rules didn't apply to him. His ability to constantly be the question and his extreme, unrelenting curiosity were things he infused into the products he created. His ability to see beyond reality to different possibilities, and his awareness of Apple's core customers' skills, needs, and desires, were part and parcel of his expanded zone of awareness.

In 1997, Steve Jobs closed a presentation describing Apple's core customer's state of being and aspiration:

Lastly, I want to just talk a little about Apple and the brand and what it means, I think, to a lot of us. You know, I think you always had to be a little different to buy an Apple computer.

When we shipped the Apple II, you had to think differently about computers. Computers were these things you saw in movies; they occupied giant rooms. They weren't these things you had on your desktop. You had to think differently because there wasn't any software at the beginning. You had to think differently when a first computer arrived at a school where there had never been one before and it was an Apple II.

I think you had to think really differently when you bought a Mac. It was a totally different computer, worked in a totally different way, used a totally different part of your brain. And it opened up a computer world for a lot of people who thought differently. You were buying a computer with an installed base of one. You had to think differently to do that. And I think you still have to think differently to buy an Apple computer.

I think the people that do buy them do think differently and they are the creative spirits in this world. They are the people that are not just out to get a job done; they are out to change the world. And they're out to change the world using whatever great tools they can get. And we make tools for those kinds of people.

So hopefully what you've seen here today are some beginning steps that give you some confidence that we, too, are going to think differently, and serve the people that have been buying our products since the beginning. Because a lot of times people think that they're crazy. But in that craziness, we see genius, and those are the people we're making tools for. Thank you very much.

Jobs demonstrated that when we choose to function from strategic awareness, miracles occur. Neither awareness nor strategy alone is sufficient. But when awareness meets strategy, it has the potential to change the world.

The unique pairing of awareness with big-picture strategy was a Jobs hallmark. In 2005, he told students during a commencement address at Stanford, "Don't be trapped by dogma—which is living with the results of other people's thinking. Don't let the noise of others' opinions drown out your own inner voice. And most important, have the courage to follow your heart and intuition." His legacy cannot be ignored, especially by those who benefit from modern technology and those who value real, honest-to-goodness design. He will be remembered as a business visionary for a very long time.

How Can You Become More Strategically Aware?

There are six simple practices that lead to the expansion of strategic awareness. They require no great amount of brainpower, no particular level of education, and little exertion or effort.

1. **Question everything.** Ask questions that challenge conventional norms and standard practices. Questions will allow you to have awareness of the big picture and explicit insight into the situation at hand.

2. **Embrace change; be flexible and spontaneous.** Be willing to look at what you can do that will generate different possibilities. Be prepared to take risks, manage these risks exceptionally well, and don't let opportunities pass you by.

3. **Cultivate a sense of curiosity, awe, wonderment, and amazement.** Remain open to the new, the unfamiliar, and the unknown all around you. Be curious about your customers, partners, stakeholders, and what is happening in the world.

4. **Constantly expose yourself to new experiences.** Learn to think differently about everyday things. Practice looking at common situations and common problems in novel ways. Observe what is happening in related industries.

5. **Be open to all possibility.** Choose to be ever aware and mindful, ready to shift strategy and tactics as the situation requires. Be willing to be vulnerable. Place yourself in unfamiliar surroundings or in the midst of unusual experiences.

6. **Be willing to step outside your comfort zone and preconceptions.** Let go of your habitual mental routines. Take notice of chang-

ing conditions around you, especially anomalies. Consider what is occurring in the national or global environment and look for implications for your sector or organization.

In closing

This book has provided some information and insights to help you recognize that there is a way to generate something totally different in your life and in the world. We invite you to try these practices for yourself. We can say with confidence that everyone on this planet of ours can make the choice to become a conscious leader and create different possibilities for the world.

It's very challenging for most people to embrace the undefinable nature of infinite choice and infinite possibilities. Yet this is a space in which leaders can truly be the catalyst for different possibilities.

Choosing to become a conscious leader and expand your awareness is up to you. If you choose it, you have to be willing to become more aware, more flexible, and more strategic. You have to be willing to become aware of the limitations—willing to overcome the hurdles that create limitations and barriers to what is possible for you. You have to be willing to rise above all of the conclusions, assumptions, projections, expectation, and judgments that are so prevalent in the world today. If you realize you can receive the judgment of the sceptics, if you are willing to be vilified and judged, then you have total freedom to choose.

Our wish is that you will build upon the inspiration from this book for any future business or organization you create as part of a new paradigm.

Please don't let other people's points of view and opinions diminish your awareness. Are you willing to receive and acknowledge that it is truly possible for you to develop and expand your capacity to be a catalyst for change? By making the deliberate choice to be a conscious leader, you will become the catalyst for a different possibility in our world. Don't let another day go by without taking action to become a conscious leader. The ability to lead with conscious awareness has never been more important than today.

It is my honor that you chose this book. I am very grateful for your choice and your willingness to seek different possibilities. A better world starts with you and me.

What counts is not the mere fact that we have lived. It is what difference we have made to the lives of others that will determine the significance of the life we lead.

—NELSON MANDELA